HOW TO THRIVE IN A WORLD OF UNCERTAINTY

8 Ways to Unleash Your Power

KARUNA S. NARAIN
Award-Winning Author

10-10-10
Publishing

How to Thrive in a World of Uncertainty: 8 Ways to Unleash Your Power
www.thriveuncertainty.com

Limits of Liability and Disclaimer of Warranty
The author and publisher shall not be liable for your misuse of the enclosed material. This book is strictly for informational and educational purposes only.

Warning – Disclaimer
The purpose of this book is to educate and entertain. The author and/or publisher do not guarantee that anyone following these techniques, suggestions, tips, ideas, or strategies will become successful. The author and/or publisher shall have neither liability nor responsibility to anyone with respect to any loss or damage caused, or alleged to be caused, directly or indirectly by the information contained in this book.

Medical Disclaimer
The medical or health information in this book is provided as an information resource only, and is not to be used or relied on for any diagnostic or treatment purposes. This information is not intended to be patient education, does not create any patient-physician relationship, and should not be used as a substitute for professional diagnosis and treatment.

Publisher
10-10-10 Publishing
Markham, ON   Canada

Printed in Canada and the United States of America

Table of Contents

Dedication vii
Foreword ix
Acknowledgments...xi

Chapter 1: Live with Passion 1
Who Are You? 3
What Do You Really Want and Desire? 5
Trust Yourself and the Universe 7
Your Authentic Self 9
Be Creative 11
Live with No Regrets 14
Have Fun and Be Happy 17

Chapter 2: Feelings and Emotions 21
Acknowledge Your Feelings 23
Assess Your Stressors 26
Manage Your Stress 29
Tap into Positive Feelings 33
Step Outside Your Comfort Zone 34
Believe in Yourself 37
Self-Care 39
Find Happiness 42

Chapter 3: Health and Wellness 45
Physical Health 47
Social Health 50
Psychological Health 52
Nutritional Health 56
Spiritual Health 59
Intellectual Health..61

Chapter 4: Life Is Constantly Changing **65**
Your Power Within 67
Don't Waste Time 70
Set Goals 73
Adapt or Perish 76
Become Your Own Finance Manager 78
Be Resilient 80
Embrace Technology 83

Chapter 5: The Power of Your Heart and Mind **87**
Flight or Fright or Freeze 89
The Power of Self-Discipline 92
The Power of Saying No 95
Perseverance 98
Be Kind to Yourself 101
Learn to Let Go 103
Focus Your Attention 106

Chapter 6: The Wonders of the Unknown **111**
Welcome Newness 113
Challenge Yourself 116
Act as a Hero 118
Be Inspired 120
The Power of Decision Making 122
Take Action 125
One Step at a Time 127

Chapter 7: Changing the Mindset **131**
Learn and Apply 133
Be Positive 136
Empower Yourself 139
Learn Not to Worry 143
The Power of Gratitude 146
The Transformation 149
Accept Failure 151

Chapter 8: The Leader in You..**155**
Be Your Own Boss..157
The Attitude 160
Your Communication Skills.....................................163
Achieve Balance 165
Manage Your Boundaries 168
Have No Expectations 171
Recognitions and Reward 175

About the Author 181

I dedicate this book to my late mother, Kamla Devi Narain,
and my late father, Peearey Narain, who loved me
unconditionally and reside in my heart.
Words are not enough to express my gratitude
for everything they did for me and my brothers.

To my brothers, Rony, Ravi, Nishal, and Suntish;
without their loving, caring, guiding, and motivating
attitudes, I would not have been inspired
to bring this book to life.

Foreword

I first met Karuna Narain at a self-development training event. At first, she was a very shy person, but after the training she was transformed into an extroverted person who showed much more self-confidence.

Karuna has become stronger and stronger with all the knowledge she acquired through her life experiences. She is very passionate about helping, and making a difference in your life.

In *How to Thrive in a World of Uncertainty: 8 Ways to Unleash Your Power,* Karuna shows you new possibilities, guides you through the path of transformation, and helps you to unveil your power to achieve your dream life and desires. This book will enable you to face your fears and accomplish greatness.

This book is designed to empower you, and help you to achieve life mastery which is so crucial, especially during the Covid-19 pandemic, when change is a constant reality.

How to Thrive in a World of Uncertainty will prepare you to face the adversity of life and show you different ways to uplift and enhance your life. You'll be so glad you did!

Raymond Aaron
New York Times Bestselling Author

Acknowledgements

To my late mother, Kamla Devi, and my late father, Peearey or "Papou," who taught me great values and ethics, making me who I am. I am blessed and honored to be your daughter. You are my heroes. Thank you for your unconditional and selfless love. I cannot say I miss you, because you are in my heart and mind. I love you to the moon and back and will always love you. Mama, whenever I close my eyes, I see your beautiful face, and you have the most beautiful smile, which I will always love and cherish. You're my inspiration, Mama.

To my brothers Rony, Ravi, Nishal, and Suntish, who have been supporting me since I was a child: You treated me like a princess. Rony, Ravi, and Nishal, you worked so hard so that we could keep going to school, with the little income you earned as children to financially help Mama. You took the responsibilities of an adult at such a young age, to look after each other, both financially and emotionally. I am eternally grateful to all of you. You have been a great mentor and role model, and always motivate me to be successful in everything I do.

Rony, you are like the dad of the house—very helpful, caring, and hardworking. I miss the awesome pizzas you would make from scratch, and all the flavorful meals you cooked. Ravi, you are amazing; you are always ready to help. I'm happy to keep in touch often. I learn a lot from you. Nishal, thanks for your continuous support. You are a fabulous cook, and you are an awesome and very organized person, and always ready to help. Suntish, you are unbelievably smart and talented. You are a wise and powerful person, just like Papa and Mama. I'm very proud of all of you and your achievements. You are my heroes too. Thank you for your continuous support; God bless you and your families. I love you guys.

To my sisters-in-law, Shyama, Sadna, and Neeta, who I consider to be like my sisters. I'm happy that we understand and get along. Thank you for welcoming me every time I visit you, and for all the different places we visited. Shyama, I will never forget how you welcomed me at your place when I visited you, with a nice warm bath ready for me, and all the delicious meals you cooked. Sadna and Neeta, you are awesome, and I will always remember our fun shopping time together.

To my nephews, Tushveen and Vihaan, and nieces, Freya, Tiah, and Preesha: You are my favorite and wonderful little buddies (even if you are taller than me), and I admire you a lot for your genuineness, cleverness, and cuteness. I wish you good luck in your future. Tushveen and Vihaan, you are both very clever and tech savvy. Freya, you are very talented, knowledgeable, and clever. Tiah, you are fun and great; your smile reminds me of my mom—so cute and adorable. Preesha, you are my little cutie princess. I'm confident that you all have a bright future ahead. I love you and miss you all. You are so far away.

To my holy or faith places, which provide me lots of peace, and help me through life. They give me strength and illuminate my path through darkness.

To WhatsApp, which connects me to my family, and to Facebook, which connects me to my relatives and friends. I am grateful for technology and your creativity. To Instagram, to share pictures and capture beautiful moments. To Twitter, for always getting the updates and other technology—thank you.

To my late, warm-hearted grandmother, Socille Narain, who was an affectionate and hard-working woman. Her love, great cooking, and her care for me, until her 90s, was very much cherished.

To my late grandmother, Bagmanea Jhoolun, who was a part of my life until her late 80s, for her unforgettable delicious meals and great stories. She was a thoughtful person, always helping everyone.

To my late uncle, Dewan Jhoolun, who had been a tremendous help to me and my siblings since we were children. He is dearly missed. His contribution and eagerness for my siblings and myself to be successful was great. He was always helping us no matter what.

To my uncle, Deonanund Narain (alias Manoon), who is a continuous support to me and my siblings, and whom I consider like my own father. You are a very nice, funny, and awesome uncle—my favorite uncle—"Chachu." To my Aunty Meemene, whom I love chatting with on the weekend; you are a very fun and lovely person. I learned a lot from you, especially cooking tips.

To my mother's sister, Morsi Meemeene, whom I admire a lot and reminds me of my mother. I can still remember how my mother would call you and chat and chat. You were both loving sisters, always there for each other.

To my uncles, aunts, cousins, and other relatives that I remember having a great time with and sharing happy moments.

To Inder R., who is dear, great, helpful, and supportive. We've helped each other in difficult times. You are a caring person with a golden heart, ready to help others in need. You are a very hardworking and generous person.

To my college friends, Reshma, Preeti, and Azimah, with whom I had lots of unforgettable fun and joyful experiences in Mauritius. Reshma, you are like a sister to me, and I love you. When I visited Mauritius, I remember how quickly your dad got me fresh coconut water from the tree, which was so refreshing, and your mama handed me all her mango and chilli pickles, which I'm fond of. I'm so blessed to have you as my great friend. We've laughed, cried, and dreamt together as one.

To my friend, Ahmad (alias Oudin), who has helped me a lot; you are a true friend. Vinod, Somou, and Natasha, thanks for being my inspiring hiking mates. Kamil, who helped me to enjoy life and be happy again when I was shattered by my first love. Sanjiv, always helping me one way or another. Rajiv (alias Da), a brother to me, always there to help. Jai, Vivian, Anoop, Marielle, Taruna, Katia, Alinee, Allan, Chabz, and other friends with whom I had fun together—thank you all for being good listeners. You all brought joy into my life.

To Lindley Couronne, I was blessed to have you as my college instructor; I was always inspired by your fairness to humanity, and your advocacy against injustice. You have been a great inspiration and influence in my life.

I'm thankful for many other friends, teachers, and instructors—of whom there are too many to write their names—during my college, university, and private training programs, who played a big part in who I am today.

To Roch Voisine, of whom I was a fan since I first heard his song, "Helene," and I kinda fell in love with him, his voice, and his songs. I was thrilled to attend one of his concerts in Ontario, Canada, but sadly couldn't meet him. Hopefully, I will one day.

To Gary, my friend; you are outgoing and so much fun, and you are so knowledgeable about investment—I learned a lot from you. I will never forget the best mouth-watering blueberry cake you baked. The video you gifted me on my birthday was very inspiring in regard to writing my book.

To my amazing friends—Shyla, Isha, Phabita, Jenny, Stephen, Giorgi, Wescar, Shweta, Alexandre, Gwen, Vaishali, Patricia, Eve, Agnes, Baber, Lizy, Karon, Maria, Raj, and Anura—whom I met in Canada and are a joy to my life. I'm so grateful for your friendship and caring in good and bad times. Rachade and Sylphide, we have spent lots of great times together, and it's a pleasure to have you in my life.

To Don, my ex-co-worker, who has been a great friend for many years now; you are a very friendly person. Isha, I love your morning quotes. It's a way to reflect and to love my day.

Peter Dunn (alias "my best friend"), I love our great conversations, always learning from you, and your delicious food. Cathy Dunn, you're my orchids expert, and I have learned so much from both of you. Thank you for treating me like your family.

To my co-workers, Brenda M., Melissa B., Fatima, Laurie, Vanessa, Das, and Lavel, who guided and showed me the path to stand up for my rights when there was lots of pressure, and also those who stood up for me.

To Ken Bower, a very considerate, fun, and athletic person, and the founder of MRAC, of which I'm so thrilled to be a member and to feel like a part of the community. From the friendship of Nella, Mattia, Hongmin, Anne, Manju, Gary, Davi, Nathalie, Mian, Ralph, Voica, Rosana, Walquiria, Sally, and others, I am able to be inspired enough to write this book. Ken, thank you for organizing and hosting MRAC hikes, and for lots of fun and social activities.

To all the staff of Centre Francophone de Toronto, thank you for your compassion and for welcoming me when I immigrated to Canada. I still volunteer as I feel like a part of the family. Stephen Beaupré, I still remember how you helped newcomers to feel at ease with your patience, your care, and your guidance. Thank you CFT for the citizenship program, which helped me in obtaining my citizenship, and for all the services you provide to the community.

To OASIS, Dada, I feel fortunate to have met you as you bring support and compassion to women in need. Your staff, Marie-Josee, Lorraine, and others, are great and loveable people.

Ines Benzaghou, thanks for empowering women to take action. I am lucky to have your mentorship of seeing clarity.

To Culture Link: Having different programs for newcomers offers opportunities to volunteer and socialize. I've also attended some settlement programs, thanks to proximity. Thanks, Rubeen, for allowing me to be a volunteer with the

NEAT program. It's a pleasure to give back to the community.

To La Passerelle-Ide, where I meet people to cook and eat together as a family, as I'm fond of cooking. Also, thanks for the programs you offer to the communities, which is really awesome. Thanks to your staff who does a great job.

To Workers Action Centre, of which I'm a proud member. Thank you Deena and the staff; I love the work you do, helping the vulnerable workers fight for their rights, and fighting for decent and fair wages in this expensive city. Your staff are welcoming and empathetic, and are always helping each other.

To Across Boundaries, thank you to Ian, Jai, the staff, and the clients who welcomed me. I learned a lot from you guys and the Canadian workplace experience.

To Syme, at 55+ Centre, it was a pleasure and most memorable workplace experience in Canada. Thank you, Scott McDonald, for your guidance and for being a friend to me. You are the most generous and awesome co-worker I've ever met. You are an IT genius, and your vision is like super power. Thanks, Nancy, for all the fun times, and for organizing meet up events despite that I'm no longer working there. Ivy L., the director, it was a pleasure working with you; I was always learning something from you and the members.

To COSTI Employment Services, which have programs to help newcomers with their resumes and cover letters in securing a job. Thank you for all your support.

To JUMP Etobicoke, YWCA, thank you for the support to immigrants, refugees, and others who need help. It's good to have such nice people working and providing support to the public.

To CAMH and the dedicated team, thank you for all the various support you provide to people affected by health-related issues, and the life changing discoveries from the research team to help the community.

To CMHA, thank you for always providing support to those affected by mental health. You offer various services, workshops, and other support to the community. I love the job you do.

To the healthcare workers, thank you for selflessly putting yourselves at risk, and for your hard work and dedication to the well-being of the community, especially during the Covid-19 pandemic.

To S. Nowbuth, compassionate and supportive head master of Mahatma Gandhi Institute, Mauritius, where I was honored to work and support the students as a school social worker with immense satisfaction.

To Appletree: thank you Sweety, Joy, and staff, although I was there for a short time. I could not forget the manager, Raj

Nijhawan, who was so generous and understanding, and kept his staff happy and motivated. It was a pleasure to work with you.

To Raymond Aaron, thank you for all your lessons and teachings. I am grateful that you taught me that I need to speak up and not be that shy little bird with such a soft voice.

To Tony Robbins, thank you for being such a major transformation in my life, through your YouTube channels. Every time I watch and listen to your videos, I feel uplifted in my life and I am motivated to write this book.

To Bob Proctor, thank you for sharing your knowledge in regard to the subconscious mind. I'm inspired by you to think positively, take action, and be grateful.

To Jack Canfield, thank you for your inspirational YouTube videos. I've always been inspired by your life lessons to be successful. Your teachings remind me of my dad's teachings— very dedicated and committed.

To Hassan Lakhani, for your stunning knowledge about real estate investments. Thank you for being a great mentor, an awesome friend, and for giving me great investment tips. You're always helping and protecting people, and ensuring both parties are satisfied.

To Manny Bains, thank you for being a wonderful friend; I learned a lot from you. You have inspired me to write my book ever since I met you, and you have always believed in me. Thank you for always motivating me and telling me, "Yes, you can do it, Karuna."

To Katharina, thank you for believing in me and encouraging me to learn the financial literacy program. I learned so much from the program and you. You are like a sister to me, and I love you.

To Cory Clarke, my friend, a great real estate agent in Toronto. You are an amazing person, and are always attentive to details. You always ensure that you leave no stone unturned to protect your clients and the people around you.

Thank you to CTV News, City TV, CP24, CHUM FM, Radio-Canada, Newstalk 1010 and others, for all the updates about the local and international news. There are lots of topics to choose as well. Also, thank you to the Toronto Star, Globe and Mail, and others. I love reading the news and always being up to date. You provide the community with a wide variety of information.

I may have missed a lot of friends who have contributed positively in my life. Please keep in mind that you have been a blessing to my life even though your name is not in the book.

Chapter 1

Live with Passion

*"Passion is energy. Feel the power
that comes from focusing on what excites you."*
- Oprah Winfrey

P assion is a powerful emotion or feeling; it's a strong or extravagant fondness of something or someone. It brings enthusiasm and a desire for anything or anyone. To live with passion means to have an appetite for life or to live life fully in the midst of change.

There is not one single person who is immune to the challenges we face in life. You need to know yourself enough to go through any obstacles. There are many questions that you may ask yourself to know what you are passionate about.

Who Are You?

It is about self-enquiry, of who you really are, or it could be a self-introduction, or to introduce yourself to a group of people. It is not about being single, married, a mother, a father, etc.; it's more than that. You can describe yourself using your personality traits, skills, strengths, adjectives, and so on.

Personality traits reflect people's characteristics and patterns of thoughts, feelings, and behaviours.

Before you define who you are, you may ask yourself questions to discover your personality traits:

How would you describe yourself?
What was your biggest fear?
What was your biggest achievement?

After answering these questions, you would be able to come up with a few examples that reflect your values and beliefs. It could be loyalty, sincerity, and generosity.

In a notebook, make a list of your traits.

SKILLS:

According to the dictionary, skill is an ability, coming from one's knowledge, practice, aptitude, and so on, to do something well; it's an expertise.

There are two types of skills: soft skills and hard skills.

Soft skills: A combination of social skills such as communication, respect, and empathy.

Hard skills: Skills that are taught, mostly for a specific job or trade. Examples are accounting, design, etc.

Make a list of your social and hard skills. After you determine your personality traits, characters, and skills, then you can move to the next question. I've helped many friends and clients to know who they are, and they have been very happy since then. If you want a free bonus session, please register at my website: thriveuncertainty.com.

What Do You Really Want and Desire?

As a human being, you have your perception of life when changes happen, and how to deal with them. If you want to unlock your full potential and achieve your greatest dream, you need to examine your situation to determine if you are happy with the life you are living right now, or if you need to change.

You are born into this world for a higher purpose than what you normally do on a daily basis. Some of the things are really important, and some are just daily unimportant things that give you temporary happiness. You may want to ask yourself some questions to understand what you truly want in life. Come up with at least 5 answers for each question.

What are you truly passionate about?
Where do you want to be in the next 5 or 10 years?
Are you living to your beliefs and values?
What struggle or sacrifice are you willing to tolerate to reach your goals?
What are you willing to give or give up to accomplish your goals?
If you were to die tomorrow, what would be your greatest wish?

After reflection, you will have more clarity of what your purpose is in this life. You will discover a new self that will be different from yesterday. Deeply think about these questions if need be, but do not quit on them.

When you feel that your eyes light up when you talk about your subject or something, and you feel energetic and enthusiastic about it, then it's your passion.

You should not give up on your goals even if you are faced with challenges, whether it's within your control or not. You need to always focus on your path toward your goals so that you can achieve something. Don't worry if you fail once or twice, but you need to push yourself so that you do not have any regrets later on in life.

If you are still wondering what you really want, and you need clarity, please go to my website, thriveuncertainty.com, and get a bonus coaching session with me.

As a social worker, I've changed the lives of many of my clients by doing these sessions. Some of my clients are working nowadays, and others are free from addiction.

Trust Yourself and the Universe

"Trust is the glue of life. It's the most essential ingredient in effective communication. It's the foundational principle that holds all relationships."
– Stephen Covey

You need to trust yourself and build your self-confidence so that you can do anything you want, without judging yourself. At times, you want to follow your intuitions or your gut feelings, because they can tell you a lot about what you really want and desire in life to be successful. Do not ignore your intuitions; even though they may not seem logical or practical, think about them. Does it happen to you that you do not listen to your gut feelings, and then you say, "Oh, only if I had listened to my feelings?"

When you lose trust in something or people, because of your past experiences, it doesn't always mean that the future should not be trusted. In fact, you should use that experience and knowledge to guide you to make better decisions, and to trust yourself to believe that you are in control of your destiny and you are responsible for your hard work and passion in life.

Life is not always pleasant; there are ups and downs. At some point in your life, someone may have broken your trust or betrayed you or disappointed you. You should not let that broken trust hurt you for all your life. You should take care of yourself, practice caring, and love yourself so that it boosts your confidence level and also deepens your relationship with others.

Trust is very crucial to any relationship, including the one within ourselves. It is hugely important; without trust, there's no relationship. If you find that it is hard for people to trust you, maybe try to learn some qualities that make people trust others. It could be honesty, transparency, courage, and other aspects that you may develop in yourself if you want to have a big support connection.

You will find out what really matters to you. These are very important areas for you to determine what you are passionate about, and how you can build trust for others to like what you are doing for yourself and others. It's like leading by example. Be genuinely involved in what you really want in life so that others can be inspired by you. Keep your word to the best of your ability so that others can rely on you and gain your trust. Do your best to keep your word.

Once you trust yourself, you will trust the Universe and the power of the Universe. You will start believing in its power. You will be determined to look for others who are trustworthy, and connect with them. You will feel a deep interest to listen to them. You will discover a change within yourself, and your pattern of thinking will change.

Everyone makes mistakes in their lifetime, and you need to forgive yourself for whatever decisions you made that didn't get you the outcomes you deserved. Mistakes happen; you may feel hurt, and then you'll forget about it after some time. Never quit on your goals because of trust issues. Build on the trust within yourself, or in others if need be, but do not abandon your passion in life. Trusting yourself is about acknowledging what happened in the past, and learning from it to be able to pursue your dreams.

Your Authentic Self

Your authentic self is your true thoughts, your beliefs, your feelings, and your behaviors. When you are being authentic, you know who you really are, and you are in touch with yourself. You express mindfulness of your feelings, emotions, and your surroundings. Whatever you see or do in life, aligns with your values and vision. Being true to yourself, through your thoughts, actions, and behaviors, will bring happiness to you.

In this technological world, we are constantly bombarded with media that affects or influences our lives. We cannot put the blame on anything or anyone, as we all earn our income differently. On many occasions, you may notice that social media affects your authentic self, because it portrays people as being perfect in everything they do. When you look at pictures on Facebook or Instagram, they're beautiful, and they show perfect happiness, and material things like a new car, a house, travels, food, perfect relationships, and so on. There's nothing wrong with that, but it doesn't show how people get to that point of success and happiness. Behind all the successful stories, there's hard work, commitment, and sacrifice.

The outer world sometimes manipulates your beliefs and thoughts, in the sense that it defines success by being more materialistic than spiritual or intellectual. Since infants, we are moulded into different boxes to fit into society, as little puppets to act and behave in a certain way. Although you may have your own way of thinking and your own individualism, you are still moulded to fit into society's norms. You are unique, and it's your values that define your true identity.

There are some risks associated with being your authentic self; people may perceive you as being arrogant or rude, simply because you are stating the truth. People may not accept the real you; not because of the fact that you speak the truth, but mainly because people don't want to hear the truth—they want to be praised. People may not respond well to your authentic side. You may get hurt, but you need to understand that pain so that you do not allow negativity to affect your feelings and emotions.

When you are true to yourself, you live in the present moment. You are happy, and you follow your passion anytime and anywhere. You do not have to worry about who you will please or deceive, as you are being true to yourself. You do not have to pretend or behave in a certain way to please others and the society you live in, as long as you are not exaggerating and being disrespectful. People will love who you are, and will accept both your good and bad sides. You will receive an abundance of love, and genuine relationships.

It is not always easy to be authentic, especially if you are working at a workplace where you are not feeling satisfied with the work you do. At times, you work because you have to pay your bills, and that income helps you to be financially independent. Sometimes you seek your true purpose or fulfilment at work, but instead of that, you feel a lack of energy, or you are being drained by your workplace environment or anything related to the workplace. The situation may upset you as you want to feel happy and genuine, doing a job that you truly love. But you are stuck due to your financial needs and your obligations to pay your bills.

If you want to know if you are being authentic or not, answer these questions:

Are you happy living your life?
Are you having sincere relationships?
Does your job fulfill your purpose?
Are you genuine in your social interactions?

If you want to be genuine, visit www.thriveuncertainty.com for some tips.

Be Creative

Once you've discovered your passion, get to know everything inside out. You can turn it toward your career. When you were a kid, you had lots of passions, and your life was very lively and joyful. When you grew up, you felt overwhelmed with work, family, and other responsibilities that come along, and you forgot to take time for yourself and your passion. No matter how busy you are, always find time to do something that you are passionate about, and make time for it on a regular basis.

Having a passion will boost your self-image and self-esteem. You may find some happiness outside your work, and you will live fully. It will distract you from your stress. And you don't have to be an expert in your passion if you are starting something for the first time. By practicing your passion or your hobbies, you will get better and better every time. Who knows? You may be an expert in that specific activity someday.

Job stress is a major factor associated with heart attack, hypertension, and other sicknesses. It is important to follow your passion and bring balance to your life. You will find that stressful situations from work feel far away when you are preoccupied with your passion or hobbies. If you bring passion into your life, your life will be less stressful, and you will eventually enjoy life better. Always have a balanced life, because if you do not have a passion, it means that you are not living your life as it should be.

To enjoy your life, you need to allow time and space for yourself. When you put aside some time on your daily schedule for your hobbies or your natural talents or passion, then you fulfill your dream and allow yourself some pleasant moments and stress-free time. Sometimes your passion may be free of cost, or sometimes it may incur financial expenses. If you have a talent for playing guitar, then in this particular case, you will need to buy a guitar to practice your lessons every time. Or if you love playing drums, then you will need a physical space to perform the activity, and if you enjoy walking in nature, you may need a pair of walking shoes.

With so much happening in the world nowadays, it appears difficult to pursue your hobbies, your inborn talents. You may think that you don't have time, or money to buy the necessary equipment or tools, to focus on your dream and your passion. It may be true recently, especially with financial stress from Covid-19 consequences; lots of people have lost trust to follow their dreams.

In the midst of this pandemic, with so many economic losses, it may be difficult to be creative. There are both opportunities and losses; you should not make the mistake of stopping your dream because of some challenges not within your control. You should not be affected by the internal or external factors that come your way. You should be able to learn from this experience, and build your character to persevere despite obstacles. You should always go toward your dream, and rise again to move forward in the pursuit of your talents and your dreams.

If you want to know or self-assess if you are fully living your life joyfully and meaningfully by fulfilling your dreams, then you should ask these questions:

> Are you living your dream life? If no, why not?
> Are you accomplishing your purpose in life? If no, why not?
> Is this the life that you are enthusiastic about? If no, how should your life be?

If your answers to most of the questions above are yes, then you know you are living your dream life that you are passionate about. If the answers above are no, then you need to assess or look at the source of why it is not happening. Think deeply on each question to find your answers and change your life. Remember that you are the only one who is responsible for your happiness. You may visit my website, thriveuncertainty.com, to register for limited bonuses.

Live with No Regrets

We have regrets when we are not where we are supposed to be in life, and when we do not achieve our goals. Be realistic; you don't have to quit your job when you define your passion. You can start working on your passion on a part-time basis, and then get used to it until you go full time. You may also reduce your expenses on things that don't serve your interest, and focus more on your passion. When you see that your passion is making you more income than your job, then you can quit your job and do your passion career full time.

You may also organize your house, or your apartment, and your work place. When you declutter your physical space, like your house or your apartment or your workplace, then you feel that you also have more space in your life to attract positive things. Get rid of unnecessary possessions that you don't use. Having less unnecessary items around you will create better mental clarity, thus promoting your mental health.

If you want to work on a project or your passion, do it now. Do not procrastinate to do it later or when the right moment comes. Remember, the right moment is now; do not add more time to your dreams. When you procrastinate on your passion, then it will cause stress and will affect your well-being. Do not be afraid to start something new or perform a task that you need to complete. It will increase your self-confidence and self-esteem.

Live every moment and every stage of your life that you are at. It may appear contradictory to say that, because people are normally stressed out or frustrated in any difficult situation. Do not let go of that particular moment of your life, even if you are in the middle of chaos. Rain doesn't last forever, or snow or other climatic conditions. Life is the same process; good and bad, nothing lasts forever. Enjoy the moment you are in, and focus on doing things in that moment without thinking about the future or the past.

Everyone makes mistakes at one point in his or her lifetime. Learn from these mistakes, and don't let them haunt you and stop you from progressing or finding new opportunities. Move on with your life. You will be happy to live your life from your past mistakes and experiences. It's an opportunity to teach your lessons to other people who may need them. Be thankful for any problem that comes into your life, because you will learn and grow from them to enhance your life. Once you acquire the knowledge to deal with these issues, nothing will stop you from overcoming any challenges.

Live in the present. Don't waste your time on the past, because what's gone will not come back. Accepting the mistakes will help you make a big step forward. Once you recognize that regret will not change the past, you will understand that you need to stop wasting your time and energy thinking about what would happen if only.... Be realistic, and live without repenting for anything that happened before. Listen to your heart, and make good decisions according to what you want. Don't worry about what others will say, because that's not going to lead you anywhere better. You need to live your life and know what you want and desire, without thinking about what others think of you or what their opinion will be.

Do not let other things that are not in your control disrupt you from your life pattern or your path to achieving your goals. Do not allow yourself to be tormented by change, such as Covid-19, which has affected so many lives recently around the world. Keep working on your passion and objectives until you find the results that you've been looking for. Don't take people or things for granted. Love the people around you and appreciate them.

Make small gestures of gratitude every day in your life. As you give, you will receive more.. Don't expect to receive anything in return. You can get more tips at www.thriveuncertainty.com.

Have Fun and Be Happy

"Fun is one of the most important—and underrated—ingredients in any successful venture. If you are not having fun, then it's probably time to call it quits and try something else."
– Richard Branson

From the dictionary, to have fun means to have a good and enjoyable time when you do something. Before you delve into what it means for you to have fun and to be happy, you need to know your definition of happiness and having fun. What does it take for you to have fun and be happy? You may make a list of all the things that you do to have fun. During Covid-19, lots of people were laid off, and for sure it's been a big issue affecting many lives. You may take this opportunity to analyze the situation, and probably take time to spend with your family. If you are by yourself, take time for yourself. And even though there may be social distancing, there are lots of ways to connect online.

Change may happen in different ways, and it doesn't always mean that it's negative. Some changes may be positive, such as receiving a promotion at work or getting the opportunity to travel to different countries. For some, it may be a good thing, and for others, it may be stressful. I know it's not easy, but always look at the positive side; it will be less stressful.

If you keep on having fun on a regular basis, it will promote your well-being. Research has found that having fun with others has a positive impact on people's relationships, and in developing communication. Having fun also gives people an opportunity to be creative and to connect with each other. However, having fun doesn't have to be associated with people. Fun can come from deep inside your heart, and bring you joy.

At times, you may feel stuck in life; you don't know what the next step will be, and you feel afraid or stressed out. This is a common emotional state that anyone can feel when change happens, and it may feel like there's no hope. It is of utmost importance to take care of yourself and to find time to have fun. When you enjoy a full life of abundant joy and happiness, you feel so much connection, and you can improve your relationship with your family, friends, coworkers, and others. You feel happy to keep going, and enjoy life at the same time, in spite of your daily challenges.

As people grow older and older, they tend to have less fun in their lives. With the amount of daily responsibilities, any adult may find it difficult to take time for themselves. They sometimes get too busy at work because that's the only way to earn a living and pay their bills. This person could be you, no matter your age. You forget how to smile, laugh, and have fun, or maybe to even take care of your health. You are busy working and looking after your family. By just having fun or incorporating it into your routine, you will improve relationships, and build trust and positive communication at both the personal and professional level.

Strong social relationships are keys to happiness. When change happens, and you need to isolate yourself from others, or if you get a job relocation, it's difficult to adjust to the new lifestyle, location, and environment. Having fun is important to keep you going. Do a fun activity that's on your list even though you are alone and you don't know anyone. If you are shopping for your groceries, you may have a conversation with some people around you, as long as you feel happy and comfortable about it.

I do like to balance my life with fun, and amongst the fun things is hiking. One day, after hiking with a group, the organizer had a draw for a $20 gift card, donated by a restaurant, and my name came up. I was surprised and, at the same time, very happy, to the point of jumping on my feet. Some of the people told me that they could clearly see my excitement. For me, that happiness lasted the entire week. It's not about the amount of money of the gift card; it was amazing that my name came up, and I was grateful. I won again the next time and was happy again. When you have fun in your life, and are happy about something, it will increase your energy and happiness toward the Universe, and you may receive more and more. Happiness makes you live longer too.

Life is all about fun, and continuing to have fun in your life does not mean that you are going back to your childhood or being childish. It's simple to say to be happy and have fun, but actually doing it, when you are unaccustomed, could be difficult at the beginning. Register at my website, thriveuncertainty.com, for bonuses.

Now that you have completed an assessment about yourself, to know who you are, and your desires to live with ambition and plenty of fun, you will discover how your emotions and feelings can change you and play an important role in achieving what you want in life.

Chapter 2

Feelings and Emotions

*"The greatness of a man is not in how much wealth
he acquires, but in his integrity and ability
to affect those around him positively."*
- Bob Marley

According to National Institutes of Health, emotional wellness is the ability to successfully handle life's stresses, and adapt to change and difficult times. Emotional health is the ability to be in control of your thoughts, feelings, and behaviors. It's about acknowledging these emotions and behaviors, and dealing with life's challenges on a daily basis. It's the ability to know when you are faced with a problem that needs immediate attention, whether it is support from family, friends, or the family doctor. In any crisis situation, you may feel fearful, stressed, and anxious, which often may lead to chronic health issues and financial crises. You need to take care of yourself first.

Acknowledge Your Feelings

Change happens in different ways. People experience emotional and psychological change, more or less in the same way, irrespective of their culture, education, or intellectual capabilities. You feel lots of anxiety, pain, and stress when you are faced with a precarious situation. You may start by loving and acknowledging yourself and your feelings. Once you accept yourself as you are, you will discover a beautiful life ahead of you. You will want more and more of this beautiful life.

Recently, in 2020, the Covid-19 pandemic has brought lots of sadness, fear, and pain to humanity. It has not been a positive situation for many people. Lots of people around the world lost their jobs, and their lack of finances has become a burden on their shoulders.

In almost all types of change that happens, whether it is global or not, it brings an economic crisis. We all experience feelings and emotions that affect our health. The best thing to do in these situations is to recognize your emotions and feelings at that particular moment, and to deal with them. When you realize and admit these emotions, it enables you to live a better life. Change is inevitable; if you keep fighting change, you will only increase your stress, and waste your time and effort by not resolving these issues. You cannot ignore change or your feelings; if you do, they will keep hurting you, your family, and the relationships around you.

In some cases, many people are and will be struggling for a long time with change. It feels like they are skating on thin ice, and on the other hand, some may cope with change in a faster or slower way. It shows that people have the power to deal with change. We all experience transitions in our lives that change our physical and mental health. Sometimes change occurs suddenly and unexpectedly, and it's okay to feel pain, sadness, stress, and other negative emotions and feelings. Other times, change happens expectedly, and we are more prepared to deal with it.

Every day, we are inundated with news of wars, shootings, death, viruses, and other things. No one can change how the world is going into chaos, but you can take care of yourself. You have to stand up, take action, and be able to cope with change; acknowledge your feelings and emotions, and determine whether it is good or harmful for your health, your family, and your environment.

During the time of transition, do not push away any pain, stress, or grieving that you may feel. Acknowledge the lost and then rise from it. Grow from these experiences; learn from them so that you become stronger and stronger. You may seek support from your close ones or from counseling if needed. During these negative emotions, go deep within yourself and ask these questions:

What are you experiencing in terms of emotions and feelings now?
How are you being affected by these negative feelings?
Are these emotions based on facts?
How do you deal with them?

Relax your mind, take a deep breath, and then ask the same above 4 questions by thinking in a different and optimistic way. Think of how you can boost your ability to deal with change by acknowledging your feelings and emotions. There are so many questions that you may have to ask yourself in order to understand your feelings and get rid of these negative emotions. The negative feelings will still be with you if you do nothing to resolve them. By simply acknowledging these negative feelings, it will help you by constructing positive energy. Go to my website, thriveuncertainty.com, for more questions that you can ask yourself.

Assess Your Stressors

Everyone experiences stress. Some of you know how to manage stress, while others don't, and it is a big risk factor to their health. Change doesn't always have to be negative; there are positive changes as well, such as a promotion, starting a new job or school, winning a lottery, or the birth of a child.

When major life stress comes up, it's crucial to understand and deal with it right away to avoid its negative health effects. There are five life events that are the most stressful:

- Death of a loved one
- Divorce or separation
- Major illness or injury
- Job loss
- Moving

Any or all of these could be a stressor at some point in your life. The best thing to do is to identify these potential stressors, so that you can build resilience in order to deal with them if they occur later on in your life. After you acknowledge your feelings and understand the way you feel, then you'll be able to explore why you feel that way.

When change occurs in your life, it undoubtedly stresses you and gives you anxiety. What you may not realize is that if you do not handle these stressors properly, they will have a negative impact on your health. To successfully move forward with your life, you need to deal with them and use these experiences to empower yourself now and in the future.

Once you know yourself, you'll understand the triggers of your stresses, and recognize your automatic responses. There are two types of responses toward stress: one will be automatic, and the other one will be planned responses. Every difficult situation is different, and you will adapt to your stress in your own way, using your own coping mechanisms.

We all go through stress in life, and most of the time our responses are automatic. Lots of factors cause stress that requires attention. Some difficult situations may require some thought so that you can plan and position yourself to really recognize the root of the issue, and to address it before it becomes poisonous to your health. Others are simple and don't require much thinking. The stress varies in nature.

Stress affects your life, but I'm going to focus mainly on the behavioral and emotional responses, due to their level of importance.

After you recognize your feelings, write down on a piece of paper what your automatic responses are, and how often you plan your responses. This will help you to anticipate stresses and responses. By doing this small exercise, it will help you to handle your stress, by using your past experience and avoiding the mistakes of how you respond promptly. By identifying responses before they occur, you can also understand them before they occur, and how you can increase your ability to recognize them.

Some negative responses to stress could be using and abusing substances such as alcohol or drugs, or being fearful. And if it is physical, then it could be changes in sleep patterns, or sometimes you become physically aggressive. There are challenges in every way of life, and building your ability to handle them will lead you to a successful life. Remember that everyone is different, and everyone has their own coping mechanisms to deal with different stressors. Always reach out for help when you are stressed out and cannot manage on your own. If you deny this, then it will be harmful to your health and will prevent you from functioning to the best of your ability. Never compare your stressors to someone else stressors.

When stress happens, you can take basic steps to reduce the impact on your health. My friends and clients are really happy about these steps that I recommend; I always get good feedback from them:

- Act as soon as you can.
- Take time to breathe deeply for 30 seconds.
- Be grateful for at least 2–3 things in your life.
- If you are into nature, enjoy the different ravines, rivers, lakesides, or others that your city or country has, whether it's by walking, hiking, biking, etc.
- Look at a picture that reminds you of a great time in your life, where you experienced happiness and joy.

Go to my website, thriveuncertainty.com, for coaching session bonuses.

Manage Your Stress

These days it's hard to get free time, especially when you are juggling family, commitments, professional life and so on. You become so overwhelmed that it's easy to be stressed out and frustrated. That's why it is very important to set aside time for your well-being and take care of yourself.

As previously mentioned, stressful experiences come in many forms, such as a change in job structure, disease, arguments, or even event planning for a wedding or a birthday party, which can result in emotional burden on health, especially when you are the only one preparing it. When you are living with high levels of stress, you are putting your life at risk. Stress brings lots of discomfort and a lack of equilibrium in your emotional and physical health, and creates havoc in your lifestyle. If you do not deal with the challenges in a timely and efficient manner, your ability to think clearly and enjoy life may be impaired.

Going through stress myself was a big challenge. The following stress management techniques can help you live a better, healthier and more productive life.

I used them, and found that they work really well in any stressful situation. I recommend them to my peers, my clients, and others.

Practice Deep Breathing

You can practice deep breathing by sitting comfortably with your hands on your lap and your feet on the floor. You can simply lie down and start practicing deep breathing for a minimum of 45 seconds.

Relaxation or Meditation

These relaxation activities bring a physiological change that can potentially lower your blood pressure or reduce your heart rate and stress hormones, thus making you feel better and more able to manage your emotions.

Healthy Eating

You can start a healthy diet diary where you can record your breakfast, lunch, snacks and dinner. The diary will help you to see all of your eating habits and will prompt you to adopt a well-balanced diet, which will cause you to feel better and healthier. It may also control your mood when you opt for more vegetables, fruits, and lean protein.

You may also consult with a nutritionist so that you can work together on a healthy and nutritious plan.

Cognitive Behavioral Therapy CBT

Research has found that CBT helps in managing your emotions and your behaviour, especially if you are prone to negative thinking. The therapist will help you to change negative thoughts into positive thoughts so that they don't impact your life. For instance, through CBT, you will learn techniques for coping with stressful life situations and resolving conflicts.

Get Moving

When you are stressed out, you don't feel like doing anything, and sometimes don't even want to get up. Incorporating a physical activity in your life will help you to release endorphins that will make you feel good, and therefore you can become more active. Slowly start with 30 minutes of regular exercise such as walking and gradually increase it.

Socialize

Reach out to those close to you when you are very stressed out. Spend quality time with your family, friends and anyone who you feel close to. Do not worry about being a burden to their life; open up and talk about things that stress you and I'm sure they will listen to you. Just having someone to listen to you will help you a lot in reducing your stress.

Make Time for Your Hobbies

It's crucial to set aside time for your hobbies as it will help you relieve your stress. This could be between 30 minutes to one hour on a regular basis, and could include reading a book, cycling, playing badminton or any game on your phone, watching a movie or anything you are fond of.

Laugh Every Day

When you are stressed out, nothing makes you laugh as you are thinking deeply about your problems. If you have Wi-Fi or internet access, watch some videos about anything that makes you laugh. I like watching sitcoms, or funny videos on YouTube. You could also start laughter yoga.

If you go to my website thriveuncertainty.com you will find more techniques to manage your stress.

Tap into Positive Feelings

Feeling positive does not always come naturally. In lots of cultures, when people are faced with an issue, they react negatively to the situation; they were not told to think positively. When we hear bad news, the negativity becomes so ingrained in our brain that it takes a lot of effort and attention to overcome it and think positively.

People are not encouraged to think in a positive way. They deal with the issues on their own. Sometimes they do not feel comfortable talking about their problems with their friends, or anyone besides their close family. People say that personal problems need to be addressed at home—true, but not when it's ruining your life. Look for support when required.

In lots of cases, whenever you are faced with an issue, your brain works in a reactive way instead of a proactive way. When these bad situations occur, you tend to have negative feelings, such as sadness and feeling low, and be depressed and stressed out rather than being calm and thinking positively and wisely. Thinking of being positive doesn't happen overnight. It takes a lot of effort and understanding to accept the negative emotions in regard to change. It took me some time to think and be positive. Be patient, and it will happen. Once you muster the positive energy, life becomes brighter. With this new mindset, it makes it easier to tap into positivity.

By tapping into positivity, people may get rid of the negativity or any bad emotions they are experiencing. It is important to take the time to focus on emotional well-being, to provide a better and healthier solution.

There are different ways to be positive and to develop a positive mindset. Instead of looking at a glass as being half empty, you can look at the glass as being half full. These little perspectives of positive thinking can lead to a greater result and better health. Write down a list of things that make you happy, or which could shift your mood from sadness to feeling happy. Some examples could be music, meditation, walking, etc.

When I feel stressed out, and I want to tap into positive energy, I listen to music that I love, and I walk in the park or even in the neighborhood. Go to thriveuncertainty.com for coaching session bonuses.

Step Outside Your Comfort Zone

Human beings feel safe and prefer to stay in their comfort zone. Every one of us has our own comfort zone, where we feel psychologically and emotionally happy, at ease, and in control of our environment. People don't like change because sometimes it takes away from them; and to escape change, people do nothing.

Therefore, they avoid being stressed out or feeling anxious about an unknown situation or an unknown outcome.

Life is all about change. You may fear taking risk because of failure, getting hurt, or feeling pain, but many of you have the capabilities to know your strengths and how to overcome obstacles in difficult moments that come into your life. You will eventually succeed by accomplishing something new and strenuous. A change in your life is beneficial to your health because it creates a bit of stress and anxiety, which releases stress hormones that help the brain to send signals to the body to respond quickly.

It helps to experience new things and to take risks. If you do not take risks and experience new things in life, you will not step out of your comfort zone; you will not take opportunities, and you will be missing out on a lot. By going through change on a regular basis, it provides more experience to deal with difficult situations, or transitioning that will eventually transform your life toward personal growth. It is good to push yourself out of your comfort zone, or do things that you would normally not do, so that you experience discomfort. If you are ready to take risk, and you feel a little discomfort about not knowing what's going to happen, these steps will give you the biggest rewards while struggling for favorable results.

I used to have a friend who had a good, secure job, and a nice house and a nice car, but his life consisted of just doing the same thing every day when he would get home from work. One day, I asked him if he wanted to start a new part-time business, and he said no. When I asked why, he simply replied that he was happy the way he was, and he was not comfortable starting something new.

If, one day, you don't feel motivated to start something new, you have to ask yourself these questions, and write the answers:

Have you ever done something where you really felt proud after you completed the task?
How did you evaluate your level of accomplishment?
How did you feel about it?

The answers to these questions will help motivate you to do new things and take on challenges in the future. Stepping outside your comfort zone is crucial for your personal growth. How can you expect to evolve in your life if you keep doing the same thing over and over without any change? You become like a robot, but when you challenge yourself, you rise higher and higher. When you take risk, you grow not only at a personal level but also at a professional level.

Believe in Yourself

When you believe in yourself, you realize that your emotions of fear will turn into encouragement and motivation in order for you to take action. You may have had experiences in life where you have doubted yourself, or you had experiences that resulted in consequences such as fear, loss, or pain, but that doesn't mean that you don't have to believe in yourself for achievement. Keep believing in yourself, and be positive; things will change.

Things happen in life where you may lose confidence in going ahead; it's normal, but it is just a matter of getting up from that fall. Each and every one of us believes in ourselves; however, the degree of belief differs from person to person. We all have our thoughts about ourselves because of how we have dealt with previous situations, and how we make choices in everyday life, and maintain relationships with those that are close, acquaintances, and those in the workplace.

You are not the only one who makes mistakes. We all make mistakes. Don't feel bad about your ability to do things, right or wrong. Try to replace all your bad thoughts with positive thinking, and write down a list of 5 things you are good at. Do not despair if for any reason things are not going according to how you expected them to be. It is good to have expectations; however, they may change due to the circumstances or unanticipated things that come your way. We all live in a world of unpredictability, but everything keeps moving. The world keeps moving, so we need to have steady goals set. Sometimes we have to amend the path to reach our goals.

I went through a lot of issues in my life, of which I never thought would have happened to me. I had goals, but things happened and I lost confidence in myself and society. I have family and friends who helped me get back to myself again; they made me realize that I have a lot of potential, and that I do not have to worry about the problem.

Little by little, I built up my confidence, and here I am, ready to live my life fully and stand up for my rights. I learned that believing in myself is the key to opening doors to prosperity. It will help me to progress to a higher and higher level. I was raised in a family where I was told that it is not polite to talk back to elders, or to your boss, or to people who are in a greater position. When I immigrated to Canada, I was still this way, because I was conditioned throughout my life to keep my tone low.

When things happened at work, I kept quiet and it affected me. I was angry, frustrated, and stressed out, until I became aware that in society, we have to be strong and stand up for our own rights. I had to get rid of my worry, fears, and self-doubt so that I could build my self-esteem and self-confidence back.

I can understand those who are going through the same emotional state that I went through. It's easier to say something than do it. I understand that it takes time, even months, and you need to have someone besides yourself to help, guide, and support you, so that you can grow and build your self-esteem and self-confidence. Believe me, if you do not have self-confidence and self-esteem, people will push you down, and they will always do what they can to humiliate you. Be courageous, and confront challenges; build up your self-esteem and your confidence, and know that you can do it, no matter what it takes.

Get any support you need in order to build up that self-confidence in yourself. It could be from your therapist, your family, or close friends, but keep doing it until you build yourself up stronger and stronger. Walk with your head held high, and be proud of yourself and your capabilities. Always stand up for your rights. Do not allow anyone to put you down. Everything that you have in life is a result of your own beliefs, and the beliefs are so powerful that they can change you into a roaring lion. Do not teach your kids to be quiet.

Self-Care

We are very busy with our daily lives, and we get caught up doing so many things that we forget to take care of ourselves. It is not until we've absolutely had enough of everything that we allow ourselves to take some time off from the routine. In this world of fast growth, you have to take time to look after yourself because good self-care is key to a balanced lifestyle, and it reduces stress and anxiety.

Sometimes women think they are Superwoman; they are multitaskers who think they can do everything at the same time. It is true in a way, but it also is not true, as it keeps you too busy to take care of yourself. You have to stop multitasking, and give yourself permission to take mini breaks—remind yourself that you are worth it. You can be more productive by doing one thing at a time. If you do not take care of yourself, no one else will; so, this is your time to start taking care of yourself. You have to put yourself first. Self-care is what you have to do for yourself in order to maintain a healthy lifestyle and prevent illnesses. It allows you to use your past experiences, skills, and knowledge to deal with difficult situations.

There are four main types of self-care:

- Physical
- Emotional
- Psychological
- Spiritual

In times of change, it is very important to take care of yourself with the intention of preventing illnesses, enhancing health, enjoying life, and being happy, and to learn from the knowledge and skills to keep a healthy lifestyle. Self-care is not something that you can do once in a while. It has to be on a continuous basis. Self-care is a lifelong habit; it is the action that you take for yourself and for your family to stay healthy and happy, and to maintain a balanced lifestyle in a good environment.

Self-care is not only for those who are healthy; it is also for those who have an illness and are taking care of themselves by taking their medication at the right time, doing exercise, and eating healthy foods.

During the Covid-19 pandemic, there have been many rules imposed by the municipal, provincial, or federal government to keep us safe, such as maintaining social distance, or not using playgrounds, etc. Despite these restrictions in regard to physical well-being, people came up with some creative ideas for doing physical activities in their apartments or backyards, and could still go walking, on the sidewalk or in parks, by keeping and maintaining social distance.

Self-care comes in different forms. It could be practicing yoga, doing meditation, eating healthier, and many more. You have to know which type of self-care works best for you. Think about some time in the past where you practiced self-care, and which thing worked best with the greatest results. It could be coloring books; doing brain game activities, such as puzzles or scrabble; making something new; or playing badminton.

With change, we think that we have to do our best, and give more than a hundred percent to demonstrate how good we are. Well, the situation will give you enough time to demonstrate your skills and your abilities. Don't forget to take self-care breaks, because that is very important in order for you to keep going and continue your daily activities. Make a list of self-care activities that resonate with you, and ensure that you practice them on a daily basis, depending on your task and situation.

You may incorporate one self-care activity in your routine life, and you will see how a few minutes daily can change your life.

Find Happiness

It is easy to say that you can find happiness when going through change, but it takes a while, and perseverance, to find true happiness. Happiness has different meanings for different people. For some, happiness means having a big house and a luxury vehicle, and having a fancy life. For others, it can simply mean being grateful for having good health, for being able to make use of their five senses, for having a caring and respectful relationship, and so on. Everyone has their own definition of happiness and what it really means to them.

In a crisis situation, if we do not take care of ourselves, we might fall into depression. Change can disturb our happiness. Shifting from manual input of data to computerized software, or getting a new job, can be stressful, and can result in depression for some people. Adapting and getting used to a new software could be beneficial or harmful to your well-being. Every person is different from each other.

Change begets change. Getting into university, from college, means a new environment, new friends, new instructors, and so on. Some are used to change, while others take a while to get accustomed to these new changes.

Any change brings a switch to the physical and emotional being. Someone starting a diet or going to a gym, as a new routine, brings pain and adaptation to a new lifestyle, through perseverance and commitment to achieve success. Nothing comes easy in life. It is necessary to adjust to what true happiness means to you, and to live your life with passion and fulfillment. In search of true happiness, you need to ask yourself the following questions:

What is your definition of happiness?
Make a list of things that make you happy.
How do you keep yourself happy when things change?
How would you maintain happiness?
How do you feel when you're happy?

So, these questions will help to determine whether happiness will have an impact in your life in regard to change. When you look at the positive side of life, you will see that losing your job is not the end of everything. You can spend some time with your loved ones, and make use of your free time to learn something new, while looking for other jobs. Remember that every change that happens in the world has its good and bad sides. No change happens for only good or bad reasons. By doing things you like, you will shift your focus positively, and eventually it will become a habit that you are passionate about.

The next chapter shows how change can impact your life. Adopting a holistic approach to a healthier lifestyle is crucial to keep fit and happy. You will discover some light in your own life, and how to free yourself from these negative impacts.

Chapter 3

Health and Wellness

*"The greatness of a man is not in how much wealth
he acquires, but in his integrity and ability
to affect those around him positively."*
- Bob Marley

Health is about a person's mental, physical, psychological, emotional, and social well-being. It is the state when an individual can adequately cope with all the demands of daily life. Wellness has many definitions, but it is a process of making informed choices toward a healthy and prosperous lifestyle, and actively maintaining it. It is also a dynamic process of change, development, and growth, aimed at enhancing well-being.

Physical Health

Physical health is very important for overall well-being. It promotes care to the body for optimal health and functioning. Physical health encourages the balance of physical activity, meditation, nutrition, and mental well-being, to keep the body functioning at its peak.

Changes occur in the body as we grow. When we are babies, we do everything without any responsibility, without even thinking about the consequences. Our bodies need different nutrients, activities, and receive lots of attention. When we become adolescents, we do lots of things, with some responsibilities. When we become adults, we get caught up in our adult lives—working, and having and looking after a family—and sometimes we forget to take care of ourselves, and of our physical activities. So, it is important to have a balanced life by integrating physical exercise into our daily lives.

Being physically active will help anyone to maintain a healthy lifestyle. There are lots of physical activities that people of different ages can do to strengthen their bones and muscles, reduce the risk of disease, and give them more energy. No matter how old you are, there are exercises for every age, whether it is for beginners or an advanced level.

When change occurs in your life, it is crucial to continue a life full of physical activities and exercise, as this provides opportunities to get away from the day-to-day stresses, and to maintain a productive life. Engaging in heart-pumping activities will stimulate and calm the body by reducing body stress hormones like adrenaline and cortisol. Thus, it stimulates the production of feel-good endorphins. Being engaged in physical activities daily, for a minimum of 30 minutes, can bring tremendous results. You may choose from a variety of activities, ranging from low to high endurance, such as walking, running, hiking, biking, and many others. The good thing is that these activities are free of cost—they just depend on your degree of motivation and willingness to do them.

Some of you may have some limitations in regard to physical activities. It doesn't mean that you cannot do anything. There are other activities that you might do, which can help you to keep fit, such as taking care of your mental health, nutritional health, yoga, stretches, and so on. You do not have to limit yourself with any restrictions. There are plenty of things and activities that you can do.

Some of you reading this book may think that this book does not apply to you. Maybe you cannot do physical activities due to the weather, environment, or any other limitations or restrictions for being outdoors—but physical activity doesn't have to be outdoors. You can do it wherever you are, in your house or apartment or your room. You can start by doing small, light activities, such as jumping up and down, stretches, or yoga, amongst others. You have to start slowly. Feeling pain at the beginning is normal until you get accustomed to what you are doing; keep doing it until it becomes part of your routine. There are lots of different types of exercise with many health benefits, like reducing the risk of heart disease, improving blood circulation, reducing stress and fatigue, increasing self-esteem and confidence, improving bone density, improving memory, etc.

Change is stressful, and when you are stressed out, there are lots of unhealthy things that you may unconsciously do on a daily, weekly, or monthly basis. You need to keep positive, and integrate physical activities into your daily life so that the oxygen continues to flow smoothly in your body. Visit my website, thriveuncertainty.com, to receive the bonus.

Social Health

Social health and wellness refers to the relationship we have with people, and how we interact with them. It also relates to building a healthy, nurturing, and supportive relationship with those around us, such as our friends, our family, our neighbors, our colleagues, and others. We, as human beings, are not meant to stay on our own. We need to build relationships with others, which shape our mental, physical, and emotional health.

When I moved to Canada on my own many years ago, it was a big change, and I felt isolated. I was on my own. I didn't know anyone, but I kept my connectedness with my family and friends from my country, through Skype. It wasn't easy to immigrate to a big country all alone and in winter. Then I met one friend, and later on, another one; and it continued until I had a few of them. Most importantly were the relationships I made that I could rely on in good and bad times. Making friends was an important aspect of my wellness.

According to studies conducted by the National Center for Biotechnology Information, social connections can decrease the risk of mortality, re-hospitalization, and stress-related health issues. It's important to have a supportive and meaningful social network that will allow you to develop different skill sets, which will enable you to interact in any social situations in a healthy way. There are lots of health benefits in maintaining social networks. It has been proven that people who have social support tend to have a better and healthier life than those who don't have social support or who live in isolation. Social support helps individuals in reducing stress.

With the change that has happened to the world, it is crucial to maintain a positive social network. It's important for children to have a meaningful relationship with their classmates, friends, and teachers so that they develop a sense of security that promotes good health, and therefore eliminates unnecessary stress. Change and stress go hand in hand, so it is important to manage stress and develop a plan that can help relieve these symptoms of stress.

There are different ways that you can enhance your social life, such as keeping in touch with your supportive friends and family, and practicing self-disclosure, which is a process of communication where you reveal information about yourself to someone else, pertaining to your thoughts, feelings, goals, and fears, enabling you to build trust with each other. You may also join a club, group, or any organization of your passion, where you feel safe to participate in group discussions and to practice active listening. You also get to connect with each other if you have the same passion and hobbies, and therefore make more friends.

Changing your environment, job, or school, or transferring to another location, requires some time to build up your social network. Some may be quick at this, while others may take time to build a social network. If this applies to you, it is paramount to keep in touch with your family, friends, and your close ones until you make new friends. Everything takes time when starting a new life, and to have a balanced life, so do not be discouraged.

When seeking new friends, always remember to focus on quality and not quantity. It is good to have a lot of friends, but it is important to have meaningful, positive relationships that you can rely on anytime. Always be yourself; do not change your personality to make new friends or to build your social network. Do not try to impress others to gain someone's attention and trust. Be yourself even if you are out on your first date. When you stay your true self, people will gain your trust easily, and vice versa. For more information, go to my website, thriveuncertainty.com.

Psychological Health

According to the World Health Organization, mental wellness is defined as "a state of well-being in which the individual realizes his or her own abilities, can cope with the normal stresses of life, and work productively and fruitfully, and is able to make a contribution to his or her community."

Psychological health pertains to dealing with or affecting the mind and the feelings. It can also be called "mental health." Psychological well-being is important as it enables someone to enjoy a better quality of life and thus live longer and healthier.

When change happens in life, it automatically affects mental health. Any level of stress affects us mentally and, therefore, we cannot perform to our highest standard. Our psychological well-being is associated with lower disease, stress, and mortality risk. There are lots of activities that you can do to enhance your mental health, and to also avoid developing any mental illness.

Having a positive and healthy relationship can boost your mental health, your psychological well-being, and self-confidence. It has been proven that engaging in positive communication, positive quotes, and positive action, leads to a healthier and prosperous lifestyle, and therefore enhances your mental health. There are brain games that anyone can practice every day in order to maintain healthy mental health, as well as yoga, meditation, and other healing therapy.

People who are financially independent are most likely to have a healthier lifestyle than those who rely on others for their financial needs. Change happens all the time, like being laid off, changing careers, upgrading school for advancements, relocation, and others, and they should not affect your health. Despite all these changes, you still have to take care of your mental health and yourself. Your mental health is so important that it can either elevate or deteriorate your health. No matter what happens in life, you should always ensure that you keep your mental health safe, fit, and healthy.

At my recent workplace, I went through some psychological stress resulting from being too nice and helpful and taking the French caseload of the Torontonians voluntarily on top of my assigned work duties. I felt lots of unnecessary pressure and stress from my workplace management, and due to my shy nature, I kept quiet. It was very stressful and frustrating, and I didn't pay attention to the harmful effects it caused to my health. Due to the fear and anxiety, it was difficult to concentrate professionally and personally. After several months of continuous workplace stress, I couldn't handle the stress any longer—I was sick.

When I got back to work, on the very first day, from the management meeting, I felt humiliated again, causing more damage to my health. I knew I had to stop it, but I couldn't do it. It wasn't a healthy workplace. The level of stress was high, and I didn't want my health to deteriorate. I wanted to get back on my feet again, for the love of my late mother. After several months, I felt better again, with the support of my closed ones, family, friends and health care team.

What I want to illustrate here is not to tell you my story. I want to tell you that life can be harsh at times, and that bad things can pour into your life; you can feel that life is against you. There may be people who will put you down. You may be fed up with all the nonsense. Don't allow anyone to ruin your life. You need to own your life so that you know how to handle any challenges. Always stand up for what's best for you.

Focus on the positive things that you have in your life. Close your eyes and be grateful for all the things that you possess— your five senses, having a place where you can sleep at night, or having food on your table. These little things that you often take for granted will help keep you motivated and positive even though you face hardship.

It will take a while, but you need to know yourself in order to understand what causes the stress, what the triggers are, and how you can work on yourself to get better.

You have to be mentally, physically, and emotionally well, in order to work on yourself in any workplace situation and environment. You have to do whatever it takes to be and stay healthy, because as long as you are healthy, you can perform any duties, and you can handle any challenges that come in your way. When you are unwell, you won't be able to deal with or handle any tough situation.

You may have also heard about people saying to think positive in any situation, even in the worst situation or experience. It may be true, and sometimes not. But personally, I found that focusing on the positive things can help. When you focus on positive things, it can change a lot in your life. You also have to work hard to change your mindset. Do not lower your self-confidence or your self-esteem. Always be proud of who you are and for what you can do when change occurs; in other words, you have lots of potential within yourself. My website, thriveuncertainty.com, will provide you with some more information.

Nutritional Health

Nutritional wellness is when you incorporate a balanced diet into your life, thus improving your overall health. A healthy diet is very important in maintaining a healthy lifestyle, by promoting appropriate weight, and reducing the risk of chronic disease, diabetes, or obesity. It is very important to recognize that food is an important source of nutrients for our bodies, as they are essential for growth, development, and a healthy lifestyle. If we have an adequate intake of each of these different nutrients, including vegetables, animal sourced food, fat, and others, then it promotes an overall healthy and balanced life; however, it's not a must. Sometimes it's a personal choice to be vegetarian or non-vegetarian, or it could be medically related, and upon doctor's recommendations to have certain nutrients and a restrictive diet.

Most of the time, when change happens, you may tend to save your money and buy less food. Buying less food is okay as long as you are maintaining a healthy diet throughout your life, and supporting normal growth. In this time of crisis, you might find it difficult to spend a lot of money on food; however, there are lots of options that you can choose from instead of buying fresh vegetables, and still have the same amount of nutrients in your daily consumption. If you eat the right food, combined with regular or daily physical activities, you will have a healthy lifestyle, and therefore reduce the risk of diseases, even chronic diseases.

With change that occurs regularly, we tend to feel more anxious, fearful, and stressed about the unknown or the known things that are about to come. Then we eat more. Cortisol increases appetite and can cause us to overeat. High cortisol levels from stress can increase food cravings for sugary or fatty foods, as stress is associated with increased hunger hormones, which may contribute to craving for unhealthy foods. We tend to eat more food that's not good for our health.

During my crisis time, when change happened and affected my life, I was binging on sweet, savory stuff like cheesecake, apple turnovers, and other sweet, bakery foods, especially since the bakery was not far from where I live. While I was doing research, I realized that the high cortisol levels were ruling my life, and I had to take action. I spent days at home without doing anything—no exercise, no cooking, and basically sleeping all day. Life was not easy; it took a lot to get to where I am now. What we need most to get better is support, and our own willingness and perseverance.

There are a lot of things that you can do to avoid unhealthy eating, such as keeping a food diary; having support from your family, close friends, family doctor, and nutritionist; snacking healthy; controlling your stress, doing meditation, and others. Every new habit takes time, so don't be too hard on yourself; do it gradually until you control the situation and your stress level. Do not hold yourself back from your close ones, your friends and your family, who can support you. Take time for yourself, to relax and unwind. Have an open door for new hobbies; do things that keep you busy so that you don't feel like eating sweet and starchy foods.

There are lots of benefits when you change your eating habits to a healthier lifestyle. One way of sticking to the good habits is by creating a list of advantages and disadvantages of eating healthy foods. Looking at the advantages will encourage and motivate you to adopt these new habits of wellness. These little changes will not only improve your health and give you more energy, but they will also lower your risk of health problems, and boost your self-confidence.

Covid-19 is a great example of a stressful situation where we don't know what's happening the next day. With the new measures that governments around the world are taking to keep the population safe from Covid-19, so many changes and restrictions are happening in our lives, such as visiting our close ones, traveling, the fear of not spreading or getting the virus, financial stress, and all kinds of other stresses that are affecting the lives of people around us.

A way of staying away from stress is by focusing on your goals. Keep doing things that you love and are passionate about, and introduce exercise or games as part of your routine life. Having a goal in mind will help distract you from the negativity, the bad news on TV, social media, and the bad situation in general. You will focus more on how to achieve your goals, and will spend more time doing things that you enjoy doing. You can visit my website, thriveuncertainty.com, for more information.

Spiritual Health

Spiritual health is the balance between the physical, psychological, and social aspects of human life. It provides us with a system of beliefs, faith, values, principles, and ethics. It is the peacefulness and serenity we feel with the Universe. Also, it's the moment when we find comfort and answers in the hardest times of our lives.

Spiritual wellness is important because it helps you in your search for a deeper meaning of life. It defines you in a better and positive way. When you are spiritually healthy, you feel more connected to the Universe, the higher source, and the divine power that's above you. Your beliefs, faith, and morals help you to make better choices in your daily life, and to take actions consistent with your beliefs, values, and culture. Sometimes in life, you may make good or bad decisions, and it's all about choices you have in that particular moment. Some decisions can affect your life and be troublesome for a lifetime of regret, while others could be defined as an accomplishment and the greatest choice ever made. Everything is in your mind.

Spiritual health has different meanings to different people, cultures, and backgrounds, depending on where you come from. Everyone doesn't see the world in the same way. Everyone has their own perspectives of life, and it comes from a personal point of view and is shaped by life experiences, values, beliefs, environment, traditions, and other factors.

When life is faced with so many challenges, it is important to involve your spiritual health and have a deeper connection with what's important to you in that particular moment or after. There are many ways in which you can double up your spiritual awareness, such as exploring your spiritual core, practicing yoga, thinking positively, doing meditation, and so on. Spiritual wellness doesn't necessarily mean that you have to connect yourself to God. It simply means to find peace within yourself through the connection of the supreme soul or the higher power. It is what you believe in.

You can simply start by being grateful for life, and you will notice that gratefulness will change your life. All you have to do is just take a step forward and commit yourself to do one thing at a time, and you will see the results. It has been proven that spiritual health may not cure an illness, but it can contribute to your well-being and healing. By actively engaging in yoga, meditation, positive thinking, and mindfulness, these can create lots of miracles to your body and overall health.

As I mentioned earlier, spiritual health doesn't mean religion; however, some people might believe that involving God and prayers may help in reducing pain and stress, and bring lots of calmness and peacefulness into their lives. It's all about how you feel about yourself, and what spiritual beliefs mean to you. If you have a deep connection with God, then go for it; don't change if it's giving you great and positive results. Visit my website, thriveuncertainty.com, for more information.

Intellectual Health

Life doesn't remain the same; it always changes. Intellectual health encourages creativity and stimulates mental activities. You have the potential to improve your lifestyle. Many of you use the available resources to be creative, learn new things, expand your own knowledge, improve your skills, and grow as a human being.

On the other hand, due to your physical and psychological limitations, you tend to stay the same even though you feel like spreading your wings and flying. Some people with confidence or trust issues may lose the ability to get away from the immediate environment or situation. It is not difficult; however, it takes time, and if you follow the path of building up your self-confidence and trust, you'll see the light at the end of the tunnel.

Change is a common thing in this complex world. There are good and bad things that happen on a daily basis, such as the improvement of technology, and Covid-19 as a pandemic issue. We all have our own perspectives of life. Some of you may come up with new ideas, and seek out new learning opportunities and challenges from this pandemic crisis. Others may be affected by stress, financial loss, anxiety, and depression in this same phase of life.

Intellectual health stimulates curiosity because it helps you to try new things and to understand how things work in a better way. If you want to put your mind and heart in succeeding and achieving your goals, you need to work on yourself toward openness and creativity. You need to have a good relationship between yourself and the environment around you, to grow as a human being. It may be difficult to focus your attention on your own goals, but it is not impossible, and you will gradually get better and better if you work on it. All you need is to be disciplined, and concentrate on yourself and your paths.

A very important skill is to be disciplined with yourself. When you are disciplined and determined to move toward your goals, you focus more and more of your attention on your path. By spending less time on the negative things that surround you, either through social media or through your environment, you put more energy into your goals and positivity.

Change is unavoidable in our society and around the world. In order to live a stress-free life, we adapt and integrate into this fast-paced world, through continuous learning and creativity. If you lose a close one, or someone gets a chronic illness, you can relate to research and past experience of how to take care of yourself, the family, and the situation. You will not let yourself be drained into hopelessness, sadness, and depression. You will focus on the positive side of life, and on the things that you have control over. There are different ways of building up your intellectual health.

Being proactive helps an individual to understand the situation and make decisions to keep moving forward, build on their progress, and to not let other people or circumstances get them down. You can grow intellectually by maintaining curiosity about what's happening in your environment and globally. By doing this, you therefore respond positively to these challenges. You use your knowledge and skills researching and dealing effectively with the adversity of life, without causing too much harm to yourself and your family.

You can say that you have the capacity to challenge yourself, by becoming a critical thinker and developing your skills to see what works best for you. Going through a tough time requires lots of skills and management techniques. You don't have to be perfect; you just have to get things going and manage your life the best you can. You will find some tips on my website, thriveuncertainty.com. And in my next chapter, you will discover some great techniques that you can use during change, which could transform your life.

Chapter 4

Life Is Constantly Changing

"To be more childlike, you don't have to give up being an adult. The fully integrated person is capable of being both an adult and a child simultaneously. Recapture the childlike feelings of wide-eyed excitement, spontaneous appreciation, cutting loose, and being full of awe and wonder at this magnificent universe."
- Wayne Dyer

Since the dawn of time, the world has been constantly changing, whether into betterment or faced with challenges. There has been lots of development in different areas such as health, technology, environment, and so on, promoting the lives of people. Change occur all the time, leaving an impact on people. Some could be enriching and beneficial, while others could be detrimental and painful. Our perception and intuition interpret changes in our lives as challenging. When there are too many changes in your life, you feel overwhelmed and destabilized. And that's how you have the signs and symptoms of frustration, anxiety, confusion, anger, and so on. To successfully navigate a fast and unpredictable world, you need to learn how to manage your survival instinct and creativity so that you reduce the negative impacts to your health, thus allowing you to be proactive and successful.

Your Power Within

I was born and raised in Mauritius, a tiny tropical Island off the east coast of Madagascar, or off the west coast of Australia.

I have four brothers with whom I spent my greatest childhood, with lots of fun memories.

A few days after I turned eleven, I lost my dad, and since that time, I remembered how life was tough for my mom, my brothers, and for myself. My mother worked really hard to ensure that we completed our education to eventually become financially independent. A few years later, I lost my mother, and my whole world shattered. I used to share a strong bonding relationship with my mother. It was the most painful moment of my life, a huge loss, and I was devastated. All of a sudden, I was left on my own. Fortunately, my brothers took great care of me until I moved to Canada.

Life changes all the time—getting married, having kids, separation, illness, death—and all this forms a part of life. I wasn't prepared for the departure of my dad. How would a girl know about losing her father at that age? The subject was never discussed before. From a state of shock, I managed to accept and live with it. Going through grief was difficult but not impossible. It was a painful experience that I would not want anyone to go through, especially not at a young age. At times, we are faced with hardships, and we ask God, or the supreme power, why this happens to us.

"What did I do to deserve this?" Well, you are not the only one asking that question. Many do. I've asked that same question too, and the answer is: It's supposed to make us stronger...

How? Why? These are common questions. You may be stressed out, frustrated by the situation, and not know what to do; you may be stuck, and your mind is blank.

It's very difficult, but remember that you have the power to get out of any tough situation. I took the path of not sinking, and here I am.

As I mentioned earlier, life has different stages, from being an infant to a senior adult, and death. Being an infant or a teenager does not require the same amount of responsibilities as an adult, unless life is different. There are a few types of relationships, and these are the most common ones:

- Family relationship
- Friendship
- Acquaintanceship
- Professional

Relationships have different phases at different stages, such as someone being laid off, health issues, financial issues, family conflicts, or loss of a loved one. All these eventually deteriorate the health status of the people affected, and affect the lives of the people around them.

People don't like to deal with change. Not only does it result in stress, but it increases anxiety and depression. It is important to cope with change and the loss of your dear ones in a way that does not affect your life. You can make use of the hidden power within yourself. Nothing is easy; everything needs hard work. If I can do it, so can you.

I've helped some of my friends with their relationship issues in the past, and it has been successful. It's significant to know whether the relationship is a growing one or not, and how to deal with it. Please go to my website, thriveuncertainty.com, to receive a free coaching session.

Don't Waste Time

In our lifetime, we all get the same amount of time—not a minute more, and not a minute less. Time doesn't discriminate between the rich or poor. We all have 24 hours in a day; the clock is ticking, and no one can buy time, no matter how rich you are. Sometimes we get a lot of things done, or sometimes we don't get to do anything at all. Everyone has their own perception of time, and it keeps changing as we age. For some, it may have an economic value like money; or for others, it may have personal value, like relaxation or spending time with their family and close relationships, or sometimes it simply means nothing.

Time doesn't mean anything. It's what you do with your time that matters. From time to time, you may have heard these common phrases: "Don't waste time," and "Time is precious," and so on. You know how to manage your time and do things that make you feel happy, yet you feel that time is flying. Each and every one of you strive to make the most of your time.

Sometimes you don't do enough, or you are not enjoying what you are supposed to enjoy. You believe that time is wasting.

For me, I like spending my time helping others because that's what makes me happy and gives me fulfilment. I remember when I went to university for a social work degree. Some of my relatives were not happy, but for me, it was what I wanted to do, to make a difference in others' lives. This was what mattered the most to me. People spend their days doing different things. For some of you, it could be becoming a doctor, mountain climbing, surfing, going to a gym to work out, building relationships, or working on your business. Everyone has their own preference. The most important thing is to find happiness in the things you do regularly. Everything is fine as long as you are putting the effort and time into things you are passionate about.

You may use your time to work on your self-development, or do something that you really love and have passion for. You may want to be enlightened and to succeed. It could vary from painting or coloring, to dancing, or doing something greater, like being a coach or a business leader, or an engineer or CEO. You will know yourself enough to know what you really want. If you have trouble, then you can refer to my chapter on "Live with Passion," where you will discover who you are and what you really want and desire in life. If you are still struggling with your passion, don't hesitate to visit my website, thriveuncertainty.com, where you can register for a free coaching session with me.

If you are in any relationship that you are not happy with, whether it's intimate or not, it is advisable that you have open communication with the person, and be honest with them so that you can both mutually discontinue the relationship. It is not good to waste your time on something that you are not happy with, or to let the other person waste their time as well. Do not worry about what will happen when you stop a relationship; just focus on making good use of your time. The same principle applies to your goals; do things that are aligned to your goals. You will yield more satisfaction.

Lots of you want to be healthy, wealthy, and so on. If you do not put your effort, energy, and your time into doing things that really matter to you to reach your goals, then you are wasting your time. If you want to be a manager of a company that you love, you can speak to another manager about how to get there. But if you keep dreaming about it and doing nothing, then you are not using your time efficiently. Probably, once you reach a certain age, and when you look back on life, then you will realize all the opportunities that you missed, and all the things that you knew were wrong, but you didn't do anything to change your circumstances. Yes, this is life, and you had a chance to change it for the better, but you didn't do anything. Do not wait for more time; it will never come—do it now.

If you want to be successful, and you want to accomplish your goals, the first thing to do is to get rid of anything that's wasting your time. Once you get rid of these things, then you'll be able to keep moving forward until you accomplish your goals. Every second of your life counts, so don't waste time on any activities that don't make you grow and don't give you happiness.

We live in a world of fast technological growth, and sometimes we are sucked into social media, which really doesn't help us in achieving what we want to do. Social media is a good way of connecting us with family and friends, but sometimes it's a waste of time when you spend hours scrolling through pictures on Facebook or Instagram, reading quick updates of everyone's lives on Twitter, and reading emails of subscriptions to media. The best way to efficiently keep in touch with social media is to control how much time you spend on it, because time flies, and you won't even notice it. If you don't want to waste your time, surround yourself with positive people and anyone that will help you grow and be productive. Visit my website, thriveuncertainty.com, for bonuses.

Set Goals

Having your goals in mind keeps you motivated about reaching something in the future, where you can feel proud when you achieve it. It keeps you motivated until your dreams turn into reality.

Lots of people don't have goals, simply because they don't set any goals in life. I have met people who said they work really hard but they don't seem to get anywhere. I do agree that time goes fast, but this is only an excuse that you can easily make up without even thinking. If you don't have any goals, it's only because you haven't spent enough time thinking seriously about what you really want and how you would like your ideal future to be.

You don't have to wait for free time to set some short-term goals and long-term goals. Once you find out what you want to achieve, then focus on doing it through your hard work and commitment. I did a training years ago on how to set SMART goals, which I put into practice and also showed my clients when I was working as a school social worker. It works extremely well as it changed the lives of many students at that school, which resulted in less school absenteeism, and they were motivated to learn and grow.

You do not have to wait for change to happen for you to set goals. You can be anywhere and still set goals, and have a good plan on how to achieve them. The basic principle is to have SMART goals: Specific, Measurable, Attainable, Relevant, and Timely. The plan should be realistic so that you can be motivated to achieve them within a time frame.

You can set goals in different aspects of your life, such as personal, professional, financial, physical, and others. You may set goals on a professional level that could potentially increase your income and success in life. You can plan and create a to-do list of how to work toward that particular goal, as there are different ways to achieve your goals. Once you have a plan, you can review it as you progress.

During change, your goals will still be the same; however, the plan may change slightly depending on the type of hardships you're going through. Do not allow yourself to quit your goals, because that shapes who you are and who you will be in the future. Keep focusing and reviewing your plans according to your means, on a regular basis, until you achieve your goals.

It is important to express your goals in a positive way. I remember one time when Raymond Aaron told me, "Don't think of a pink elephant." Then he told me to close my eyes—and guess what? The first thing that came into my mind was a pink elephant. So, you can do it, and you'll see it for yourself. It's called the power of positive thinking.

When you have a lot of goals, it is good to achieve them one by one. You may give each of your goals a priority to avoid being too overwhelmed. Therefore, focus all your energy and attention on one goal at a time. It will keep your motivation up, to continue or pursue the next goal. Here are some tips I can give you before you plan your goals:

- Don't set goals that are too easy or too hard for you to accomplish.
- Ensure that the length of time to achieve them is enough for completion.

- Amend your plan if necessary.
- Visit my website, thriveuncertainty.com, for additional tips.

Adapt or Perish

I moved to Canada few years ago for a better life. I was looking for a change in my life, and I had some goals. Immigrating to Canada is a lengthy process but a rewarding choice due to its abundance of opportunities. My immigration process was not an easy one; however, what kept me going was my goals of what I wanted after settling in Canada. I was thirsty for a new beginning, a new life, and a new journey.

Although it was an unknown country, I was ready for my new adventure, as it had what I was looking forward to. Having my goals in mind made it easier to follow and not be distracted.

It felt like a honeymoon period when I first came to Canada. Everything was beautiful. I explored cities and their sites, such as Niagara Falls, Kingston, the CN Tower in Toronto, and so on. There's no harm in visiting many places. It's a big country, so why not have some pictures to send to your family, friends, and others.

Then came the interesting part of being in a new country: getting a job or continuing education, and children's needs and education. Well, that's part of settlement, and when we plan these things in a systematic way, they are easier to get through and to get them done.

Even though some workplaces may ask for work experience, do not worry; it will come with time and patience. So, don't be too hard on yourself. You might alter things and take any job to get work experience in the new country, and then move to your dream job, if you still want to. I took this path and it worked.

With the Covid-19 lockdown and its consequences, it might take longer in Canada, the United States, England, or any part of the world, to get a job; so prepare your mind to be patient. Focus on the "now," and on getting a job eventually. Take time to relax even though it looks impossible, and everything will come on its own. Below are some simple tips for before and after any move, whether within the country or to another country:

- Research what your goals are for the country or location you want to be in.
- Prepare yourself mentally.
- Look for accommodation of your needs.
- Make a strong cover letter and a resume.

There are so many things that you can do to achieve your goals in a timely manner. You may connect with me through social media or email, and I will give you some advice. If you follow the path of success, you will find it. It may be both a stressful and exciting experience, but later, when you will look back at your path, you will feel a great level of satisfaction and completion.

I believe that adaptation and being mentally prepared is important to the process of immigration. Do not despair; keep on working toward your goals. One day, you will feel proud of yourself and your achievement. I've helped many people navigate the path of settling in Canada, and they were happy that I made the path easier for them. If you want more information, please go to my website, thriveuncertainty.com.

Become Your Own Finance Manager

With the global economic crisis, financial situations can deteriorate over time, and our health will inevitably be affected. We live in a country where everything has a cost to it. Nothing is free. We pay for the basic necessities of life, such as water, food, clothing, and shelter. Depending on if you live in a developed or developing country, the amount of money you require to buy your basic necessities will differ. However, you will still need money to live and to have a healthy lifestyle.

There are many factors that contribute to financial loss and stress. For example, if you lose your job and you have your mortgage or rent to pay, then it's both a loss and a stressor, which affects your health, family, and social relationships. There are things that you can do if you lose your job. You can start a business, depending on the situation. You have to bear in mind that the income you receive from the business may not be enough to pay the rent, but it helps. The best thing to do is to protect yourself, your family, and your children, financially, so that they do not suffer any losses if anything should happen now or in the future.

I came across a lady who introduced me to a financial literacy program, which I had never learned at school. During the Covid-19 lockdown, when online courses were ruling across countries, I learned a lot from the financial educational program. I learned how to ensure that I have proper protection, and to make money work better for me; I became my own money manager.

I cannot deny that Covid-19 has brought lots of frustration and pain to the world. However, looking at the positive side of things, this pandemic has enabled lots of people worldwide to learn online and improve themselves. It also comes with meeting the right person at the right time. Since childhood, I was always into self-development, and always increasing my awareness and expanding my knowledge. I grab opportunities that fit into my purpose for achievement as they come.

A shortage of money is a big frustration and is stressful to your health and wellness; but if you focus on the stress, you will never find ways to earn more money. You will just be wasting your time and energy if you don't focus on the right direction and path. It is important to direct your energy toward the right path, so that you are in the flow of receiving more income. It is crucial to always stay on track and to stay focused. Stop the bad habit of buying excessively. Start with new habits of saving. Change doesn't come easy; it takes discipline and action, and a strong desire for achievement. The more you desire and want to change, from deep within your heart, the more it will become doable, and the easier it will be, until it flows within you naturally. For bonuses, visit my website, thriveuncertainty.com.

Be Resilient

According to the dictionary, resilience is "the capacity to recover quickly from difficult situations; toughness." And according to the American Psychological Association, resilience is defined as "the process of adapting well in the face of adversity, tragedy, threats, or significant sources of stress, such as family and relationship problems, serious health problems, or workplace and financial stresses." As much as resilience involves "bouncing back" from these difficult experiences, it can also involve profound personal growth.

Practicing mindfulness is a very important tool for cultivating resilience. In challenging times, like the Covid-19 pandemic, it is important to manage your mind so that you increase your ability to cope, and be better prepared for any change or pandemic problems. By analyzing your own thoughts, you will have more skills in place before another calamity strikes you.

Change occurs everywhere. Some countries have natural disasters that destroy everything. Life is not easy, but you have the power to adapt to any situation and be stronger and better. Change is not within your control, yet you have the ability to adapt and face it anytime. When people are faced with any hardships in life, it causes a lot of emotional distress, and by being resilient, you involve behaviors, thoughts, and actions that anyone can learn and develop to maintain a healthy life with less emotional consequences.

Anyone can become a resilient person by overcoming challenges and problems. You can respond constructively to any hardships, and remained focused even when the worst happens. You can appear as a leader because you stay positive, work well under pressure, and motivate yourself, your family, friends, and others to keep going. That's how someone should be to balance his or her life, and to be resilient when change happens.

Being in an economic and financial crisis may increase fear and stress in lots of people. By building your resiliency, you will be able to treat all your problems as a learning process, thus having the necessary skills to handle a crisis and develop realistic goals, for now and for the future, so that you don't fall into the same trap if something similar should happen in the future. By taking positive action and nurturing a positive view of yourself and others, you will grow from your fall.

Generally speaking, human beings do not like change because it causes lots of stress when an unknown thing is about to happen. Not knowing what the outcome will be, increases your feelings of being anxious and nervous. You do not have to think that way; even though the worst may come, no one knows whether it will be a good outcome or not. Being anxious doesn't help. As the proverb says, "Don't count your chickens before they are hatched." It means that you shouldn't depend on or make plans for something that hasn't happened yet.

It takes some time to shift your mindset and your perception; it doesn't happen overnight. You need genuine support and guidance to embrace change. Below are some skills of resilience that I use and also suggest to my friends, which really work for us. You might use them if you are faced with a challenge:

- Accept the change of whatever it is.
- Build positive social relationships and support, and stay connected.
- Talk about what you're going through.
- Remain calm and live in the moment.
- Practice self-care.

By practicing these skills of resilience whenever an emergency hits you, it's like building a muscle that intentionally focuses on the core components above, to withstand and learn from difficult and traumatic experiences, and overcome the challenges. It takes a lot of practice to get better.

When you identify your areas of irrational thinking, then you will lose that tendency to catastrophize these difficulties, and adopt a more balanced and realistic thinking pattern, meaning that there would be a change in your mind and thoughts of how you interpret and respond to them. Go to my website, thriveuncertainty.com, for bonuses.

Embrace Technology

Technology has created many mind-blowing discoveries, and it has changed the world in many ways. We are privileged to be living in a world where science and technology move fast and make a big difference in our daily lives. Some improvements are: traveling within countries, self-driving vehicles, global communication, entertainment, and others. Technological innovation has its good and bad points for your personal and professional lives. Despite changes, there are still many of the aspects that remain constant. You may need to focus your attention on the good things so that they have a stabilized effect on your mind, body, and spirit. As long as you use technology in the right way, it will enrich your life, but when technology is misused, it affects people's lives and those close to them. It could also worsen their lives through laziness, isolation, and no socialization.

The Covid-19 pandemic had millions of confirmed cases, and thousands of people lost their lives. It has been a heartbreaking and painful time; however, on the other hand, millions of people have recovered, thanks to medical and scientific advancements. They can still live with their families and friends, in happiness and prosperity. Moreover, science has paved the way for developing new vaccines and other drugs to help people on a daily basis with their illnesses. It has enabled lots of people to stay alive, and to be healthy and spend time with their family and friends.

During Covid-19, the development of technology has been so beneficial in many ways, whether at a personal or professional level. Many workplaces enabled workers to work from home, and children were able to continue school online, with what is called virtual learning. People have gained massive knowledge and awareness during covid-19, through online learning that is accessible worldwide. Technology has been a tremendous help to lots of users, in facilitating their online workshops, education programs, meetings, celebrations, and so on. Single people living on their own were able to connect with many people all at the same time online, thus reducing their boredom. Making time for and fostering relationships with family and friends, creates a sense of security and socialization.

Technology keeps improving, and there is more to come to make our lives better and better. There are so many advantages of technology. For example, you can file an online application, pay your bills, verify your banking, and make investments, as well as many other things, from your couch at home, or anywhere around the world, with internet access. Some people may like online learning, and some people like in-class learning.

Everyone has their own preferences, and that's fine. You can read my book, in hard copy or e-book, or download some information from my website, thriveuncertainty.com.

You are accustomed to what you are used to, and there are different modes of education available in your country. If you are not used to virtual learning, allow yourself time to learn; take your time until you adjust to the new type of learning.

In life, nothing comes easy. When change happens, it doesn't look at your skin color, your religious background, your age, and so on—the whole society is impacted, just as in the recent Covid-19 pandemic. If you have a problem or are faced with a challenge, you may want to analyze the particular problem from different angles and perspectives to find the solution that works best.

I know it must be frustrating and depressing, and causing anger, anxiety, and more. I know how it affects you because I've been going through the same phase; but believe me, the best thing to do is to look at the positive side of life and change the way you perceive things. It's not easy and will take time, but with practice, you'll get it. Get into the habit of always looking at the bright side of life. Now, if you go to my next chapter, you will be happy to learn a lot about the power of your heart and mind. When you apply this to your life, you will notice transformation—you will grow from it.

Chapter 5

The Power of
Your Heart and Mind

"Life is a song - sing it.
Life is a game - play it.
Life is a challenge - meet it.
Life is a dream - realize it.
Life is a sacrifice - offer it.
Life Is Love - enjoy it."
- Sai Baba

L isten to your heart, as it will show you your true path toward your goals. Do not reject your intuition, as it is part of your beliefs and values. Use your powers to achieve your purpose in life. Do not doubt yourself and your imagination. Believe that you will achieve your goals, no matter what it takes. The power of your heart and mind will conquer all negativity.

Fight, Flight, or Freeze

We live in a world that consists of evolution and chaos at the same time. There is global financial collapse, emerging markets, political unrest, technological innovation and more. Everything is new and changing at the same time. What's new today can be outdated tomorrow. There's no guarantee of what could happen overnight.

The term fight or flight or freeze refers to your physiological reaction when something terrifying occurs, whether it is mental or physical. The physiological or psychological response to stress prepares your body to react in the face of danger. The response is triggered by the release of hormones that prepare your body to react to the dangers by either fight, flight, or freeze.

When you are faced with a particular danger, you can feel your heartbeat racing and your entire body becomes tense and ready to take action or run away. You may choose fight, flight or freeze, meaning that you cannot fight the situation or flee from the situation and your mind goes blank.

Whenever change happens in society, your body automatically responds to it. When you cannot respond to it, that's where it's called either flee or freeze.

To determine these two responses, you may ask yourself some questions.

What are my physical responses?
What are my physiological responses?
Am I able to respond in a calm manner?
Am I sweating and shaking?
Am I making it up in my mind?
Are they real threats or dangers?
Am I able to deal effectively with the threat?

At times your body responds automatically to phobia and fear, which may not be real. If someone is afraid of bugs, anything and everything that's about the same size as a bug will scare the person, and they may react in the same way as real fear. Your body might experience heartbeat and respiration rate increase because the response doesn't realize which fear is real and which is not.

In a perceived threat, your brain has an automatic response in regard to fight, flee or freeze. You may need to see the source of the danger or the threat so that you know how to deal with it as soon as you can, and protect yourself. Once you are able to determine the type of fear, you'll be able to react and respond accordingly.

When change happens, whether it's a natural disaster, workplace change or any other change, you will need to control your emotions so that you know how to deal with the change effectively. For example, if there is a tsunami, then you need to evacuate as soon as you can; if you are in a workplace relocation, then your body and your mind will work together to adapt to the new changes and new location.

Your body can also react to stresses that are not life-threatening, such as work pressures and family issues. When you are set on your journey towards your goals, you may feel overwhelmed. Sometimes, you may want to pursue more education in your field, and the exams may scare you. If your fears paralyze you, your fight or flight response will take place because of the fear to prepare and plan your future career. You may chill out and think in a calm way, practice meditation or spend time doing what you love as a hobby and then get back to your plan, and your mind will be able to think productively.

When you are the only income earner of your family and you get laid off from work, you will definitely experience frustration, depression, anxiety, and financial loss. Your immediate goal will be to gain another income so that you can support your family financially. You will do everything you can to earn an income so that you can feed your family. You do not flee the situation, but rather you come up with new ways to help yourself and your family.

The Power of Self-Discipline

The Oxford Dictionary defines self-discipline as "the ability to control one's feelings and overcome one's weaknesses; the ability to pursue what one thinks is right, despite temptations to abandon it."

Self-discipline is one of the most important life skills to develop, as it keeps you going. In the midst of crisis, when it's difficult to keep track of what's happening, it's important to learn how to be self-disciplined. It will help you in accomplishing your short-term and long-term goals. When you learn to be self-disciplined, you will be able to make wise decisions, and then persevere with actions that will result in being successful. Even if you are not successful at the beginning, do not quit; keep doing it until you get into the process of continuously moving forward.

No one is born with self-discipline; you need to develop and learn how to do it efficiently. Do not worry; no one becomes self-disciplined overnight. It requires a lot of effort and sacrifice to take control of yourself and your actions. Sometimes, due to the level of discomfort, and because of your fear, you are reluctant to be self-disciplined, and you put it aside to be accomplished later. Once you practice and exercise being self-disciplined, you will discover a lot of benefits, and it will become part of your life.

Self-discipline can overcome laziness, indecisiveness, inability to take action, and procrastination. When you acquire the skills of self-discipline, you will be able to take action even though it requires effort to do it. It will also help you to be creative and do things that you have never done before, because you have the willpower to learn and grow. You will discover having more patience, compassion, perseverance, and a better understanding of how things will work. As you get more and more into this mental strength of taking control of your life, you will set more goals and take steps to achieve them.

If you do not develop this self-discipline, it will affect your health, your financial status, your social life, your personal life, and your professional life. Once you realize that you are creating more stress in your life, you will have the desire to get rid of these challenges. The reason may be fear of the unknown, or that you believe it is difficult to get through it. Once you develop a pattern where you see yourself taking small actions regularly to reach your goals, you will push yourself so that you can get better and better over time. All you will need is just a little bit of practice every day, and perseverance or guidance, until you master self-discipline.

Self-discipline is not a difficult thing; however, because people run from the discomfort, they do not handle problems, and therefore they procrastinate on getting the difficult task done. If you want to succeed in life, you have to learn the skills, habits, and all kinds of attitudes of self-discipline, so that you can take action in a timely manner. If you tackle your problems right away, you can then take the burden off your shoulders. But if you ignore the problems, they will keep increasing, and as long as you don't get them resolved, they will create stress in your life, which will eventually have a negative impact on your health.

When change happens in your life, it is crucial to be self-disciplined so that you can take control of your life, instead of the change taking control of you. If you are just starting to be self-disciplined, you might struggle at the beginning to get things done. As you keep practicing, and take control over your life, you will feel better by being able to cross things off your to-do list, by getting things done instead of having to deal with them later. When things are postponed, they don't get resolved until later; and if a problem arises from it, it makes it a lot worse.

When I immigrated to Canada, my first goal was to get a job; however, being someone who loves to travel, I was always traveling from one place to another. Then my savings that I brought, started to be depleted. I became self-disciplined; I tailored my resumes and cover letters, and within three months, I had applied to more than 200 jobs. At one point, I was frustrated because I was rejected for having a lack of Canadian working experience. Then I finally got a job, which eventually brought me to my field. When you have self-discipline and the willpower to get something that you want badly, you will have the mental strength that is required to do the things that need to be done, and you will resist any temptation that may get in the way of achieving your goals.

I have helped some of my clients build up their inner strength, and increase their mental strength, to overcome laziness and procrastination. If you want the skills to stick to your decisions and follow them through without being distracted, visit my website, thriveuncertainty.com, and register to get the free coaching bonuses.

The Power of Saying No

Everyone has the right to say no. It's a small word, but it has lots of power, and sometimes it may feel awkward as it has some negativity attached to it. In some cultures, people feel uncomfortable saying no, as it implies refusing to perform or to give something. You should not feel guilty about saying no, because it is your fundamental right to say no to anything that you do not feel like doing, or which you believe will hurt you or your well-being.

We live in a complex world that's constantly evolving. At times, you may feel overwhelmed with so much going on, and you will need time for yourself. When you say no to people, it is your right, not a privilege. You should not feel guilty about not accepting any offer of work when you are exhausted. When you have a clear vision of your goals, then you will give them importance, and you will only say yes to the things that you really love and want to do, and which align to your values, ethics, and goals.

There is no shame in saying no. You don't owe an explanation or an excuse to anyone, unless you are at work and it is your responsibility to perform certain duties on top of your primary roles. When you say no, it also means that you are standing up for yourself. You do not have to take any unnecessary pain in life. You deserve to be treated with respect. You do not have to allow others to lower your self-esteem, nor do you have to allow yourself to be hurt by any relationship that brings you down.

You have the right to end any hurtful relationships, and to take responsibility for your own life.

When I was working as a caseworker in Toronto, Canada, I accepted the manager's request to voluntarily provide services to the francophone community, given that I was fluent and proficient in French language, on top of my assigned work duties. I love my job and felt lucky to be a Caseworker as it was my dream job.

Then I became overwhelmed by both the English and French workloads. After several unsuccessful attempts to get management help, and due to the level of stress, I said that I could no longer do it. It wasn't an easy decision, but it was the best thing to do at that moment.

But, if I had said No to voluntarily provide French services to Torontonians since the beginning, then all this stress would have been avoided. I was the only certified French caseworker at my workplace to help all the Francophone in the big city of Toronto. I was happy to have the support of several co-workers, who helped me in those difficult times, as well as the union and other people that provided me with continuous support.

You don't have to be like me and only say no when your life is at stake. I know that it was my basic fundamental right to say no, especially when I was hired as an English caseworker, and not a French or bilingual caseworker. I realized later that this was the consequence of being too nice, or not being able to say no; but I learned and grew from these bad experiences.

Throughout my life, I've always been helping others; maybe that's why I'm a social worker. I get lots of satisfaction when I can help someone and make their life better than before. Now that I learned my lesson, I know when to say no and when it's not right.

When we are stressed out, we have a high level of the hormone called cortisol, and we crave for sugary or sweet stuff.

We know that it is not good for our health, and therefore we need to say no to these sweet foods. It is not easy, but it's feasible, and anyone can do it. Sometimes you may go to a party or a buffet, and because you paid the price for the buffet, then you are allowed to eat all the food you can eat, even though you feel full. Well, it is true, but it may not necessarily be the best option to have. If you focus on a nutritional lifestyle, that's where you need to say no to so many foods, even if you only go there once in your lifetime. It's such a powerful word, and sticking to your values is very important. You may visit my website, thriveuncertainty.com, for more information.

Perseverance

The Oxford Dictionary defines perseverance as "the persistence in doing something despite difficulty or delay in achieving success." Perseverance is the power to follow through until you achieve your goals, dreams, and vision. Everyone faces challenges in their lifetime, and they all learn from these crisis situations to grow and do better. The more challenges you face, the more you learn from your mistakes and are able to overcome any difficult situation. Life is not simple, as we live in a complex society with growing innovations.

I met with a City of Toronto caseworker during my settlement in Canada. I was looking for a job in my field of social work, while working as an assistant to the executive director in another company to gain Canadian experience. My workplace experience was the greatest experience I had in Canada, together with my awesome colleagues. However, I had my goal to become a caseworker, and I persevered until I became one. It's not an easy path, and I kept applying for the same position even though I was rejected twice. It's not about good benefits but the satisfaction I yield when I make a difference in someone's life. As I immigrated to Canada as an immigrant, I can therefore emphasize, to the newcomers, the importance of reaching their goals.

When you persevere in life, and you are confident about getting the job you want the most, or the goals that you want in your life, there's nothing that can stop you from achieving it, except your own mindset. Perseverance is the key to many doors of opportunities. When you feel stuck but want to get through a difficult situation, do not quit. Be curious to learn how other people survived that same circumstance, and overcome the difficulties. You can reach out to them to see how you could reach your goals through their experience. Get support from others. There are lots of people out there who are willing to share their experience so that you can apply it to your situation. If you don't find the people because you are new to the city, town, or country, don't panic; just Google the question, and you will get lots of answers.

If you want to persevere in life, always have your goals in mind. Do not get distracted by minor things that don't lead you toward your vision and your dream. Go for it even though the path may seem to get longer and longer—it may feel like the more you do, the longer it appears. It happens, not because of your lack of patience, but because you want to find results soon. Be patient, and you will eventually see the light at the end of the tunnel.

You may be working for a company for many years and then you get laid off. You may think life is unfair to you after so many years of hard work, and you ask yourself if that is how you get compensated for hard work. It may be a blessing in disguise for you to be able to start something on your own or get a better job. It may be a new beginning for your new career or your own business, which you have put aside for so long. But you finally have the opportunity to start your dream work, where you can put in the same effort but with more productive results. You can now persevere to reach your goals in your own company and be the one in control, and make more progress.

Sometimes, if you've been working for many years in a management position or high-level position, your ego may stop or prevent you from seeking support and connecting with others. Humans need connection to survive, especially in difficult times. Many of you may feel strong and think that you will overcome the obstacles by yourself. It may be true, or maybe not. Seeking support from your loved ones or the people you trust, doesn't put you in a vulnerable position; it helps to connect and to share your experience with others, to gain support or suggestions and more ideas.

We all get discouraged at some point or another, but it is that inner drive that keeps you going and keeps telling you that it is not time to quit. At times, you may ask yourself what the point is of going on.

Some people take months or years to reach their goals. That doesn't mean that you have to take the same amount of time to reach your goals. It means that you have your own way of doing it, and everyone is different. Remember, all successful people have gone through challenges and failures at some point in their lives. You just need to keep going until you are successful. Patience is crucial when you start something new, in many situations in life.

Be Kind to Yourself

The world is changing fast, and there is hardly anything in life that is not changing. Along with this change comes fear, frustration, anger, anxiety, feelings of insecurity, curiosity, opportunities, and so on. We experience a lot of negative emotions attached to change. People tend to forget their own happiness and start judging themselves and others. They try to be perfect, and they feel pressured by parents, peers, co-workers, and management to keep pushing and doing their best.

Everyone makes mistakes; no one is perfect to the point of not making any mistake at all. Don't punish yourself or others for making mistakes, because this is how you learn and grow, to be better or achieve another result. If you are participating in a competition, there's no harm in doing your best because you want to win a prize or a trip or a reward attached to that competition. But if you are not in a competition, and you want to achieve the goals that you have put aside for a long time, do it regularly and steadily, but don't be too harsh on yourself. Listen to your heart and mind when you are about to start a new activity or start a new business. By having a detailed plan to follow, it will help you to combine an action plan together with happiness, meaning your hobbies that you keep doing on a regular basis. Take time to think positively about yourself and the work that you do. You may even reward yourself after achieving each phase of the path toward your goals. You may treat yourself to a nice dinner, a spa, a trip, a long ride, or anything that you would love to have, if you accomplish a particular task.

At times, in this complex world, you do a lot of things for your children, your family, your work, and for the people around you, except not for yourself. Start incorporating self-care into your life, especially during difficult times. Take a nap when you feel tired or when you feel you need some rest. Have a balanced meal and enough sleep so that you can be in a good mood and in a good health condition. Practice self-compassion toward yourself by being kind to yourself; understand your emotions, and genuinely feel better in the moment—not as a means to fix your pain, but to feel happy. When you feel happy, you will want to keep doing what you want to do, and you will have an open mind and see new opportunities instead of seeing only challenges and negativity.

There are lots of struggles in life that we constantly go through on a regular basis. It does not mean that we are being punished for whatever happened in the past. It simply means that these struggles will help you gain enough resources to better manage and take care of other obstacles or challenges in the future. Life is not a bed of roses, because even roses have thorns. Go to my website, thriveuncertainty.com, for more information.

Learn to Let Go

We all have gone through some hardships in our lives. We don't want to hold on to them; we want to let them go so that they don't poison our present and future lives. Our past creates who we are, but we can't let it define us or hold us back. When you hold onto past pain, it doesn't fix anything. In lots of cases, especially when it comes to the past, all you have to do is accept the past and let it go—that's the best thing to do if you want to move on with your life. Letting go of painful emotions and feelings is not easy. At times it may takes months or years to accept and get through it. The earlier you let it go, the better it is for your health and well-being.

When you hold onto hurtful feelings, it doesn't only affect your well-being; it holds you back from creating your identity and reaching your goals. Once you let these negative feelings go, you will feel lighter, and you will have a great sense of relief from an unpleasant emotion about your past. Then, at that point, you will be able to move forward and create your true identity of who you really want to be and what you want to achieve.

If you are in a hurtful relationship, you don't need to justify this relationship with a past one; just let it go. If you were rejected before or were being abused, or have any painful feelings from a past relationship, if you don't let it go, these memories will keep tormenting you, and you will not be able to see the beauty of life. You need to let go of that negative relationship and enjoy your life. Focus your energy to live positively and happily on your own so that you can attract happiness into your life.

Sometimes you may feel scared and anxious to let go of a hurtful relationship, because society, your culture, and other people will point fingers at you, even though you may be the victim. There are many steps to letting go and moving on. If you keep holding onto these negative relationships and feelings, they will eventually develop into depression. You need to talk to a person you trust, or a therapist, about how you feel, and they may help and support you with the process.

Sometimes people are deeply hurt, and they cannot forget these emotions and feelings. They cannot forget people who hurt them and caused them pain. It doesn't matter whether it's a close relationship or not; you need to let go and start on a fresh page. Do not wait until it's too late to recognize that these hurtful emotions and feelings will prevent you from growing and achieving your dreams. Forgive them now for any pain that they caused you, and move on. When you end a bad relationship and create space for a new one, you will see that life is different and beautiful. Don't be scared to let go and attract new vibes.

Letting go of negative feelings doesn't happen overnight, especially if you've been holding on for a very long time. When you focus on moving forward in life and happiness, you will remove pain from your life, and you will be controlling your mind to develop positive feelings, and empowering yourself to climb up the ladder.

When you're dealing with obstacles, plan to take some time out. Do something different, or rest. Later on, you can continue dealing with the challenges that you are facing. When you have a big plan and big dreams, acknowledge that you might make mistakes sometime. Do not hold onto these failures and prevent yourself from achieving your dreams. Keep moving forward.

The process of letting go and moving on from a poisonous relationship can be stressful and painful. You should not ignore yourself and your needs. This is the moment when you practice self-care and ensure that you maintain a healthier diet and lifestyle than before. You may engage in new hobbies so that that you keep yourself busy and happy. Take care of your needs and desires, and put all your attention on yourself for some time, until you feel ready to live by yourself and be happy.

You cannot change the other person, so don't waste your time and energy thinking that you can. Don't think that by doing everything for the other person, he or she will change. Do not limit yourself; keep believing in yourself. Truly believe that you can accomplish your goals by yourself, and that you do not have to rely on other people, who hurt you, to complete something. Open up your mind, believe in the good things around you, and feel powerful and be grateful for every moment you breathe. Do not take your life for granted. Your life is precious.

Focus Your Attention

The world keeps evolving because people want a better life and future for their children. Change is fundamental to the Universe. If there were no innovations and new ideas, there would be no progress, and therefore life would be boring and aimless. When you act and execute on your plan, you get either good or bad outcomes. When you obtain good results, you feel motivated to continue until you reach your goal, but when the outcome is bad, then you need to change the plan and act accordingly for better results.

Lots of people in life are not focused enough to have their full attention on their tasks. By being this way, they do not encourage their peers, family, or others in a positive and enriching way. It's good to eliminate or reduce distractions around you, like the movie being played on the TV, or checking social media or emails from time to time. When you stay focused, you will be productive and get things done quickly. But being constantly distracted will prevent you from reaching your goals. You will have to put more effort and time into getting things done, and eventually this may create discomfort, especially if you find other people reaching their goals before you do.

People keep on procrastinating because they are afraid of the unknown outcome, or it appears difficult to them, or it's a long process. Avoiding the completion of the task doesn't lead you anywhere. It will increase your anxiety and frustration, and make you feel uncomfortable when you think about the task. If you find that focusing your attention on a specific task is a difficult step for you, then you can apply some techniques to motivate yourself to take action. You may break your goals into smaller steps that you can achieve in a timely manner, as you are the only one who knows your potential and how much you can do in a day or in a week.

It is true that sometimes you may not feel motivated to focus your attention on your assignment, but don't put it for one week or one month. It's important to understand that change and success are an ongoing process, and it doesn't happen overnight. It takes time to be successful, but only if you take control of your life now. You will have to sustain your focus to become more productive and achieve your dreams. The more you keep performing, the more routine it will be, until it develops into a habit. Focus on your path until you are satisfied with the results you obtained and expected.

It's never too late to act on your dreams and your goals, even if you have had them for a very long time. It's better late than never. If you find yourself in a position where you need support in whatever task you are doing, do not hesitate to ask for help; because if you don't, it will be harder for you to complete the task by yourself. Nowadays, there are lots of free YouTube videos that you can access to boost your motivation to perform your activity that energizes you, and to take action. Be confident in what you know and what you believe you can achieve. Your psychological state will drive your commitment to achieve your goals.

Being fearful is a common emotion that keeps you from being focused. Do not hesitate to speak to your close ones, or to get a mentorship program from those who have been successful. You can follow the same path and be successful too, with their guidance. You cannot just click a button to get rid of your fear or your frustration of not focusing. You will eventually overcome your feelings of discomfort when you focus more and more without distractions, but it takes time. If you still find yourself having lots of difficulty staying focused, then you may ask yourself these following questions, and the answers will allow you to take the steps.

Why is it important to complete the task?
Will it help you to enhance your life?
Will it help you to make progress in your life?
Is it something that you can avoid postponing?
Is it something that you need to do right now?

After answering these questions, it will help you to determine the importance of acting. You will commit to act on these tasks, which you already analyzed, and you can break them into small steps to reach your final destination. For bonuses, go to my website, thriveuncertainty.com.

My next chapter will help you with new things in life, and with creativity. It will expand your knowledge and ideas.

Chapter 6

The Wonders of the Unknown

"Life is a gift, and it offers us the privilege, opportunity, and responsibility to give something back by becoming more."
- Tony Robbins

No one knows what's behind the unpredictability. If you do not venture or take the chance to know what's behind the next door, then you will not know whether it is great or not. It's only when you step into the unknown that you'll be able to see the beauty.

Welcome Newness

How do you feel about change? Are you worried or excited about change? While some changes are overwhelming, worrisome, and fearful, others are welcoming. Every one of us has our unique perspectives of change.

Immigrating to Canada was a big change. It was exciting and, at the same time, challenging. It took time to settle down, to get the job in my field, to make friends, and so on. On the other hand, the first summer months were like a honeymoon period. I traveled a lot to visit new places, and it felt like an adventure—I discovered new places, architecture, and attractions.

During the Covid-19 pandemic, lots of changes happened in our society, in the country, and worldwide. We, as human beings, have our own personalities and our own ways of adapting to change. We have the power of managing the situation and accepting the environment as it is. By doing this, we stop fighting or resisting change. When we are confronted with challenges, we develop our skills and experiences, and we transform our lives to higher levels, both personally and professionally.

Change provides an opportunity for us to do something new, and to grow and evolve with these challenges. Some of us may have the habit of doing the same thing on a daily basis; or sometimes, due to a lack of time, we don't have the opportunity to do something new. So, now is the time to do what you have been dreaming of doing—what you are passionate about. Do not let this opportunity go by. Do it now—do not postpone it, even for an hour—it's your moment. The clock is ticking.

I left my country, my family, and my friends, in search of a better opportunity. I was looking forward to this new adventure that had lots of potential to improve my life, and where I could learn a lot to have a prosperous life. I cannot deny that there were ups and downs; however, I was focusing on the positive things toward a greater purpose and life.

It's true that Covid-19 has done lots of harm to society, and has even taken the lives of many people. Lots of businesses have closed down, people have been laid off, and so on. If we focus on the negative side, we will never see opportunities that it brings. We need to be open minded in order to see the opportunities that it brings to us. People are able to work from home, there is less traffic on the road, technology has improved a lot, and there are more learning programs online, along with many more opportunities being out there.

Every situation or event has its pros and cons. Sometimes it takes a bad situation to happen for you to change your life. These tragic events are the turning points in your life that lead you to something far better than what you had before. A divorce could be bad at the moment, but it was so that you could meet the perfect person. You may lose your job now, only to get a better job later on, or to start a business. Never think that what happens to you is bad; it's a way to seize the opportunity from it, and to grow. It may be the discovery of your life purpose, and your personal growth.

If I had not gone through these challenges in my life, I would have never written this book. Always be curious to make new things; be creative, be enthusiastic about change, be open to new ideas, and be in the spirit of growth and abundance. If you toss a coin, there are two outcomes: heads or tails. It works the same way with any situation in life; the outcome is to accept or not, and the choice is yours. Every attempt toward your goals is a new way of getting there. If you live in a particular area and want to get to a place that is 500 miles away, there are different ways to get there, such as taking a bus, driving there, or taking a cab, a plane, or a motorbike. The choice of how you get to your destination is yours. Go to my website, thriveuncertainty.com, for more information.

Challenge Yourself

Change can affect a person in many ways; however, if someone wants to grow stronger from it, then the best way is to take the challenge. Anyone, irrespective of their age, can take it at any time so that they master their own destiny. Changes happen throughout our lives, no matter what, and we cannot always control them. We can use our skills and experience to handle these situations.

With every change that happens, there's always room for positive growth and learning if we focus our mind on positivity and work through it. When you take action and challenge yourself, you prove that you have the capacity and discipline to overcome these situations. When you complete these tasks, it shows your ability to accomplish something in life, and boosts your self-confidence. That's how you grow from these situations to the next level. You can be proud of yourself for the actions you took and the accomplishment. The result is only an outcome, and any outcome could be good or bad. Never be hard on yourself if it's a bad one. It only means that you have to amend the route toward your goal by doing something different from what you did earlier. Never be discouraged by the result of the first action.

It may be stressful to do something when the outcome is unexpected, but the most important thing is that you did your best and persevered until you found a result. As I mentioned earlier, results may not always be positive. At times, they may be negative or unsuccessful, but you have to keep going and never stop doing it.

Doing something amidst change helps you to clarify what you really want to achieve in life. It keeps you moving and concentrating on your goals and the path to do it. It is a good way of distracting your mind from listening to the negative media surrounding you that gets you down. In times of crisis, social media tries to center more on the events surrounding you, and therefore you tend to focus your attention on the events rather than the solution and the path.

It may take a while to decide what things you would like to do if you haven't worked on yourself. Take some time and write down things you would love to do, and then you can implement them. If your attention or focus starts to fade, take a small walk, or do something different from your goal and then get back to it.

When you feel that challenging yourself is stressful, yet you want to go for it, then start by taking baby steps. You may have to take action to increase your self-awareness and self-confidence, and learn from your experience to improve your life. It could be anything, like painting or doing some coloring; or for others, it could be starting an online course in the field of their future dream career, or being an entrepreneur. It could be anything that would distract your mind from the negativity, and align to your goals and dreams.

Taking a challenge is not always easy; it requires determination and perseverance. It will eventually improve your personal and professional growth, to deal with any challenges that may come your way, now or in the future. Go to my website, thriveuncertainty.com, for bonuses.

Act as a Hero

When I was a kid, I always wanted to be a hero, like in the movies, to save the world. I'm sure that each and every one of you, in your lifetime, wanted to be a hero of your choice, whether it was a cartoon hero or not. Unknowingly, you have the power to believe and do anything you want to. When you were young, it didn't matter how difficult the situation was; you didn't think about how you would get there, yet you were behaving and acting like a hero.

There has been no big change since you were a kid until now. If you really want to be a hero, then you have to initiate the change you want to see in yourself. You need to take action and implement it right away. You have to make use of your skills and adapt to change. Life is not constant, and if you don't act now in regard to change, then you will remain the same.

Lots of people have competences and character, and therefore, when you combine both of them, it makes you who you are and what you are capable of. If you are good at reading, writing, and speaking, then it's a great asset that you possess. For those of you who have good planning and communication skills, then those are your bonuses. When you add your character, which may be that you are responsible and authoritative, it leads to a balanced life, where you can take action to tackle situations in your daily life.

We are all heroes in life. Some of you may be a brother, sister, parent, grandparent, or anyone who has a lot of responsibilities toward others. It could be raising children or grandchildren, or nieces and nephews, or looking after the family, working to support the financial situation at home, or helping others. You are already an unconscious hero. You all need a little push to do more of what you do on a routine basis. It's about doing things that really have a sense of achievement and purpose for yourself. It's where you feel proud of the accomplishment and the outcome that it provides.

When I was young, I was in great appreciation of my mother's effort, her dedication, and her love for my brothers and myself. She was my hero. She did everything in her power so that my brothers and I would have a happy life. She was committed to making sure that we have a proper education to eventually be financially independent. Against all odds, my mother accomplished her mission. She's my hero. I also understand that we are the savior of our own lives, our own hero, and we need to take actions to reach our goals.

Dealing with change in a timely manner helps you to feel strong about yourself, in the moment and in the future. It can also be used as an example for those close to you, and for others, to follow their paths in doing whatever they have the potential to do, and to discover themselves and their strengths. They can use these strengths to live in perfect harmony with themselves and the people around them. You have lots of potential yourself, and you can make use of those skills to reach where you want to be. The sky is the limit if you want to achieve anything in life. Visit my website, thriveuncertainty.com, for bonuses.

Be Inspired

Everyone at a certain point in time goes through difficult times. You all have had your moments in life where everything goes wrong, and change occurs in a negative way. All this happens for a reason: You grow from these difficult times. Many of us want to arise after falling apart. Sometimes we gain our inspiration from those close to us—our parents or people who've gone through the same situation as we have, and great celebrities who succeeded the path of growth, like Tony Robbins, Richard Branson, and many others. They are all like us. Some may not even have had the luxury and the comforts of life that we have, yet they struggled and were committed to have a better life, and they reached their goals. Some of you may not have a luxurious life, and may not even have food to eat, but you should not let yourself be limited by your circumstances.

You can do the same thing to reach your goals, using your skills and your potential that you have in your mind and heart. By putting it into action, you will find the result sooner or later. Time will determine the outcome. We are inspired by people who feel better in themselves, are strong and dedicated, and who persevere. They have the courage to push through fears and continue with their dreams. They are firm with their beliefs and commitment to reach their goals. They are courageous and will fight till the end.

Gratitude is key to those who want to make a difference, in their lives as well as that of others. People who are full of love and appreciation are not afraid to be open. They believe that when they give more, they receive more, and therefore they are happy to share and help others. If you are inspired by those who have the same vision as yours, then you would also want other people to follow your lead, and therefore be a great example to your friends, family, and those you want to inspire.

You may change your physical environment if you feel that you want to get more inspiration. At times, you might feel discouraged or disappointed with everyday events, so by changing your environment, you get less distracted and could think clearly. Some may want quiet places, while others may not.

Change is associated with stress, and once you master your mind, and have clarity for your purpose, you can achieve anything you want. You need to have a clear mind of how you can achieve your goals, and a clear picture of your life to get results. If your mind is always distracted by things going on in your environment, in your life, or in any situation of your life, then it will be difficult for you to have a clear picture of what you want.

If you feel that you do not have a clear picture of your goals, wants, and desires, then you may need to think about spending time with a mentor and having a conversation about your goals and how you can pursue them. It will not be an easy task, but with the guidance of your mentor, you will see a big change in your life, and you will be inspired to grow and have a better life.

Covid-19 may have brought the world to a halt, but your life has not halted. If you do not get inspired by people, then change your situation or environment to change your life to a better one. Never stop dreaming. More information is provided on my website, thriveuncertainty.com.

The Power of Decision Making

Every moment of our day, we make decisions. We have choices, and we need to make decisions of what we want. Sometimes those decisions we make are small and inconsequential; sometimes those decisions are major and life-altering. There's lots of power when we decide, even if it's just choosing what type of clothes to wear or what we eat on a daily basis. Everything we do, eat, or make is based on our decisions. Our life's outcome is our daily summary of the decision-making and actions we take.

According to the dictionary, a decision is defined as "the act of or need for making up one's mind." Based on unctv.org data in 2018, it's estimated that the average adult makes about 35,000 remotely conscious decisions each day. We all have many options in life, and we make the wise choices or decisions with positive or negative outcomes. Some of you choose to wake up early and start working on your personal and professional goals, while others may prefer to wake up later and hang out with their friends whenever they are not working or busy with their daily activities. It's all about decision making.

Not all good decisions have a good outcome, and not all bad decisions have a bad outcome. We may think that a bad outcome was the result of a bad decision; no, it may also come from a good decision. Do not be too hard on yourself if a bad outcome is the result of your decision. It just means that you need to look at different angles before you make the next decision. You always learn from your previous experience for a better result.

"A person who never made a mistake never tried anything new."
– Albert Einstein

When you have clarity about your goals you want to pursue, it is good to sit down in a calm state, and consider all the factors and the values that you could bring to the process before you make your decision. It is a state where you feel that both your heart and your mind are in harmony with the decisions that you make; it's a feeling of comfort and acceptance and belief. It is also where you feel that your decisions are aligned with your core beliefs, your vision, and your goals. You may even ask yourself if this decision will help you move forward based on your values.

Before I made the decision to immigrate to Canada, I did a lot of research about the Canadian lifestyle, careers in my field, accommodations, living expenses, and so on. The decision was not simple, and it was not easy to leave my family to immigrate to this big country. I know about the weather in Canada and the different provinces. I thought about everything, and then I made my decision and filed my immigration application.

Making the right decision can also be frightening; therefore, people prefer not to make any decisions, especially when they don't know what the outcome will be. Even though there is the freedom to choose, it's still scary. People can make decisions where they may make lots of money, meet their dream life partner, and be successful; or on the other hand, people's decision making may negatively affect their lives by losing money, which affects their family and relationships.

We live in a society that is so full of options that our brains feel overwhelmed. If we need a new set of clothes to attend a party or event, we go to the store, look at the different choices, and due to so many options, we find it difficult to make the right decision about which outfit to buy. It is a tough one.

You are confronted with a wide set of options, the environment, and personal choice and public opinions, and sometimes you just want to have the best outfit at the event. Decision making is not simple for everyone. Some may make a quick decision and stick with it, and others may not. Everyone has their own perspectives on decision-making. There is no right or wrong answer; everyone has the freedom to choose based on their beliefs and values. Don't be afraid to make a decision. Visit my website, thriveuncertainty.com, for bonuses.

Take Action

Taking action is defined as "doing something or acting in order to get to a particular result." It is important to decide what you want to do in your life; however, taking action is determined by your willingness to change and act for a better result.

Earlier, I gave you my example of when I made the decision to immigrate to Canada based on my research and other things. What got me into this country were the actions and steps I took after making that decision to immigrate here, which was filing an application for immigration, and all the processes I went through to get here. Taking action is very powerful, as it gets you to the place where you want to be, reach, and achieve in life.

Change is stressful and causes your brain to be blocked, and your thoughts to be suppressed. If you want your dreams to manifest in reality, then you need to bring these goals into actions. Lots of us have had opportunities to do free online courses during Covid-19, but if we do not take action to implement this in our lives, then nothing will change, and we will still be the same as we used to be. If you want change, you need to take action now. You cannot wait for another day to change, or procrastinate on things you can do now.

Sometimes we come up with excuses, like we feel that we don't know how to start something, or we are not ready to start it now, or other excuses that we put in our way for us not to take action. Everything that you believe is hard, is in fact easy. You just need to take a few steps to reach where you want to be. Sometimes you may even postpone a simple thing like making a phone call to your friend or a business entity. It's as simple as taking your phone and dialing the number, but even these little things, people sometimes postpone. If you want to buy a bicycle and start cycling, or take swimming lessons, don't wait for next summer—start now.

Everyone has had a time in their life when everything went wrong. Do not think that bad things happened only to you. You should not fall into the trap of being the victim and thinking that you are the only one who has had the most dreadful experience of your lifetime. Lots of people feel joy and happiness in their life, and it's not because they live on a bed of roses or have the best life and opportunities. It's because they take action of what they want.

People like to collect ideas but don't implement them into their lives or their workplace. Lots of companies have great programs and trainings for their staff and management teams, but how many are being implemented into their lives and the workplace? It's good to learn about different things, but how many are actually taking action? Some people think about taking action when the right moment comes. Then they postpone it for 1 day, 2 days, 1 week, 1 month, and before they know it, it has already been a year and nothing has happened. They are still waiting for the right moment to start taking action. Does it happen to you too? If yes, you know what to do now. I've helped a lot of people to take action, which has resulted positively. You can do it too.

One Step at a Time

Change is difficult to manage at any point in time, especially when you are on your own, or a single parent or a vulnerable person. Take your time and do things slowly, at your own pace, and carefully.

When I immigrated to Canada, I made a list of things I wanted to achieve, like getting a job in my field, buying a car, buying a house, and so on. At one point, I wanted to achieve everything all at once. I thought I was a multitasker and could do a lot of things at the same time, such as juggling more than one job at the same time, socializing, exercising, doing my hobbies, and taking time for myself. I later understood that I wanted to achieve too many things, and that everything needs to be going at its own pace.

I understood that I needed to be willing to put all the necessary commitment, creativity, dedication, and time into what matters the most to me, in a priority list. I created a list of things in order of preference, and I have been doing my best to achieve most of it. I do one thing at a time, and I believe it will get me to my goals, slowly but surely.

During change, when you feel overwhelmed with lots of things happening, the best thing to do is to take it step by step, and you can increase your tasks as you get stronger and more comfortable. This will give you motivation to do more and more until you complete the whole task. If you do ten things at the same time, then you'll be dividing your attention into so many things and getting nothing done. When you put your energy into doing one thing at a time, you'll yield lots of satisfaction. There is no one-size-fits-all process to perform a task; everything must be designed and tailored to fit the unique needs and things you want to achieve. Do not fix a problem by using a method that doesn't adapt to the problem.

When you deal with change, whether at a professional or personal level, there needs to be trust. It is good to trust yourself or the task that you'll be doing. It is good to trust others so that you can share the job or do it together as one. With change happening all the time, trust plays an important role in life and is crucial so that you can rely on others anytime. Change can happen for the better or for the worse.

You should not let change take control of your mental and physical health. When you inspire trust in others, the work will be done faster without hesitation. Once there is a solid core of trust, there will be good teamwork to complete the job. Trust happens when other people recognize that their leaders or their elders are trustworthy and inspire trust. Whenever there's change, do not walk away; more than anything, work in the best and most efficient way to avoid any more hardship to anyone.

Lots of times, we want to get things moving faster than they should. It may take longer than expected if you do one thing after the other; the process will be longer, but you will eventually reach your goals. You would have to work harder to get through the process, the risk, and the suffering, but success would finally be yours. With ongoing change, you may have to alter the process, or take a longer one. You may want to quit, but you need to push further and keep moving forward until you reach your finish line.

If you go to my website, thriveuncertainty.com, you can see some examples of how you can commit to do one thing at a time and get great results. The transformational ideas in the next chapter will blow your mind. You will be amazed at how powerful you can be with just one idea.

Chapter 7

Changing the Mindset

*"It takes someone with a vision of the possibilities
to attain new levels of experience.
Someone with the courage to live his dreams."*
- Les Brown

T he Oxford Dictionary defines mindset as "the established set of attitudes held by someone." Any person can change their mindset. You may change your mindset through your powerful beliefs. What you believe today may be different tomorrow. If you want to accomplish certain things in life, it requires a strong and persistent mindset. People can be empowered and changed by watching motivational speakers on a regular basis. They can also change their mindset through ongoing personal development and of what they now believe.

> *"If you deliberately plan to be less than you are capable of being,*
> *then I warn you that you'll be deeply unhappy for the*
> *rest of your life. You will be evading your own capacities,*
> *your own possibilities."*
> – Abraham H. Maslow

Learn and Apply

We all have ambitions and goals in life. Some of us achieve them and some do not. Why is it like that? Why do some people become millionaires or billionaires? Why do some people keep doing the same job on a daily basis? The answers are not magical answers; they are factual information. The only difference between the rich and the poor is the mindset. The mind is the most astonishing creation and a very powerful force.

Change is everywhere, and it's happening on a daily basis—no one can escape it. Everyone is affected by change, either in a positive way or a negative way. Some individuals believe that they have a fixed mindset and that they are born with these talents. On the other hand, others believe that they can upgrade their skills, talents, and mindset through continuous learning, perseverance, and dedication. They believe their abilities can get better and better every day if they really work on them.

Lots of people want to be rich, yet they do nothing to get rich, while others put in lots of effort and a strong desire to learn and grow more than anything else. They believe they can develop greater mindset through hard work and perseverance. When they focus on their goals, and commit themselves to be disciplined, they find greater results and achievements.

There are two types of mindset. There is a fixed mindset, where the intelligence is stagnant or still; and there is a growth mindset, where the intelligence can be developed better and better. Anyone can learn new skills and talents. It all depends on you. If you believe you can improve your abilities and your personal qualities to grow, then do not hesitate to learn more and more so that you can grow your intelligence and your mind.

When change happens in life, people tend to avoid challenges because of its unknown outcomes, frustrations, and stress. When people have a growth mindset, they embrace challenges, because they see lots of opportunities that they can take advantage of for their own personal and professional growth. This is how you should look at challenges; it's a way for you to grow into a better person. When you allow yourself to develop a growth mindset, then you have a hunger to learn and discover new things. You will have a desire to grab every opportunity to embrace challenges and to grow as a person. Do not fear failure or disappointment; learn from it, and take it as a learning experience where you can alter the present to get better results and achievements.

At school, children learn a lot about important things in life; however, they do not teach how the mindset works and what comes with it. We learn about unlimited personal growth when we are at a later age, at universities or from speakers. When children are in kindergarten, they learn to play with logos, which help them to learn more about mathematical concepts of counting and building relationships, and working in teams, and then later in their lifetime, they learn other skills such as problem solving, critical thinking, and others. All these skills are important for their development and growth. Mindset is an important part of everyone's growth. Hopefully, developing the mindset will be introduced as part of the school curriculum in the near future.

A growth mindset reduces stress and anxiety, and improves the emotional and overall well-being. Additionally, it improves self-confidence in children and adults. It is important to adopt a growth mindset from an early age, as it will boost self-esteem starting in childhood. Children will not feel pressured or intimidated by others. It works well with shy children as it helps them to understand better that there is nothing to be afraid of, and that no one is perfect and we all have the same rights.

Visit my website, thriveuncertainty.com, to register for my free coaching session.

Be Positive

In the simplest way, to be positive means to have a positive attitude and to think in a constructive way. It is where you are optimistic about things, situations, events, and interactions around you. By being positive, you can have hope for situations to improve, and you become stronger to tackle any difficult situation that you may encounter. Having a positive attitude helps you to be more productive in your daily activities. It also helps you to accomplish your goals in an optimistic way, even though you may have lots of bumps in your path.

By being positive, it enhances your life. Staying positive in a complex world of crisis could be challenging; however, being positive helps to reduce stress and enables you to make the right choices. It also promotes your mental well-being and immune system. Remaining optimistic when you are impacted by the current state of things, especially during the Covid-19 pandemic, where you have been in lockdown for months, is not easy. Businesses are closed, there is no job security, people are being laid off, and there are fewer social activities due to isolation and social distance rules. It's crucial to stay calm and hopeful. Many of you are also skeptical about positivity; it almost feels impossible to be positive when there's so much negativity going around in the world. You have to stay hopeful that everything will go back to normal.

In the midst of all this upheaval, it's important to see the positives, and any opportunities that anyone can come up with. People who were laid off can spend more time with their family, be proactive, learn new skills, or start a new hobby; or they can create new ideas to start or develop a business that will benefit people during this pandemic, or during change in general. It also gives the opportunity for people to work from home, thus avoiding the risk of contamination, and there is less time spent commuting.

By staying calm, you help the mind to relax and to find solutions to get out of this predicament. If the brain is too distracted by social media and the chaos in the environment, then it will be difficult to think and act appropriately. It will create more stress for your mind and your body. Eventually, instead of finding results and positive outcomes, it would add more stress to your ongoing stress, which could be harmful to your health, your family, and your environment.

Positivity takes practice and is not something we were born with. Scientists are now learning that the power of positive thinking can rewire our brains to overcome negative thinking patterns. Researchers have found that people who think positively, are happier than those who do not. They also found that when practiced regularly, positive thinking is a great coping strategy for tough and difficult times. Adopting the power of positivity can help you live longer and better, without any chronic health conditions, including mental illness.

It has been proven that if you keep exercising your mind to think positively, then it will improve your overall well-being. All you need to do is to remove any negativity from your mind so that you can fill it with a positive attitude. According to the Mayo Clinic, positive thinking can reduce negative self-talk and help improve physical as well as psychological well-being. Those who harness the power of positive thinking are reported to have better cardiovascular health, lower stress levels, and greater resilience during times of hardship.

Believe me, I've been through a lot, and I know how difficult it is when we have to be optimistic in a crisis situation. It's easier to say than do. We adapt to situations, and we have automatic negative and positive feelings, depending on the circumstances. Everything needs time in order to cultivate good habits. Be patient, and you will find the solutions.

Below are some tips on how you can be positive in challenging situations:

- Acknowledge your thoughts and feelings.
- Do one thing at a time.
- Allow your brain to relax; have no thoughts.
- Be thankful and be grateful.

Write all your qualities on a page, and look at them when you feel low and negative.

Remember that the chaos will pass, and everything will be normal again. Visit my website, thriveuncertainty.com, for more information.

Empower Yourself

During a crisis situation, our mental states often tend to exacerbate a crisis or a challenging situation. Our minds wander a lot "by default," and are hooked by obsessive thinking and feelings of fear and helplessness when a crisis situation occurs, like the Covid-19 pandemic.

At times, people get trapped in negative thinking, and social media concentrates more on these issues, which makes it worse. When your mind gets stuck, you begin to feel fear, and therefore it's harder to see the positive side of the situation. Once you become creative, you will see opportunities in front of you.

You want to become powerful to take control of your life, and not allow others to control it for you. When change occurs in your life, it takes a different turn, and therefore all your attention and focus is on that particular situation. By being in control, you can focus your attention on positive things, overcome challenges, and deal with mental health struggles, financial worries, and your work/home life balance.

When you feel that you need support in times of stress, and that the door is closed, connect to those close to you—family, friends, and other support that exists in the community.

The Covid-19 virus caused lots of restrictions and social distancing at the beginning, to prevent its spreading, and it brought isolation; it prevented you from seeing your friends, your family, and others. The virus is still around, and people take more precautions everywhere, whether it is at the workplace, in the environment, or external places. It is good to take control of your life by keeping yourself and your family safe from danger.

Change takes us by surprise and without notice. So, when big changes happen, we feel weak, shocked, and depressed. However, it is possible to take control of your mind during these tough times. All changes have their good and bad sides, but if you focus too much on the bad aspects of change, there will be no room to concentrate on the opportunities, or on your personal or professional growth. You may have to be receptive and grow a positive mindset to accept challenges as opportunities for growth.

To grow from change, it is critical to trust in your abilities, and to recognize that you have the power to improve yourself by putting effort and commitment toward it. You can start working on your hobbies, and the things that you enjoy doing and that make you happy. You can be empowered by what others are doing, in a good way, or empower others through your actions. You may start to focus on your long-term goals, and see different paths for achieving them if you have some free time for yourself. Or if you are busy with change, then take a moment to make some time for yourself, as you may get overwhelmed by change.

When I moved to Canada, I was shy; and at one of my workplace, I felt that my self-esteem was being lowered, only because I had expressed my thoughts about the stress that came from the mismanagement of the French caseload. At that time, I was the only certified French caseworker for that organisation, and was voluntarily taking on the responsibilities of the French caseload for the francophone community of Toronto.

Even after three French caseworkers were hired for the same position, the problem persisted. They voiced their opinions as a group, and then the problem finally got resolved. They were not shy, and there were three of them, while I had been the only one at the time. I had felt pressured by the same person, and because of her power, I didn't speak up, as I relied a lot on the financial aspect, which paid my bills.

Now, when I think about the workplace situation, it feels silly and naive to think how I could have been so quiet and let things happen. Other caseworkers stood up for their rights when they feel pressured or intimidated by the same person. I feel stronger now, and I can stand up for my rights. In life, you need to empower yourself to grow higher so that no one can control your life or lower your self-esteem. You need to muster courage to fight for your rights, and to say to yourself and to others that it is wrong to intimidate others. Even though there are human rights, lots of problems are still happening around the world. You need to assert your rights in life.

During Covid-19, when the pandemic was taking the lives of so many people worldwide, I was able to empower myself to be stronger, and to become a more resilient person. If you don't take action now, nothing will change. You need to be able to stop others from putting you down. We are all equal. Self-empowerment, or to be empowered by others, is important for your personal growth.

Sometimes you may be placed in a situation that requires you to simply do something to the best of your abilities, and to do what you have to do. When you do what you are capable of by exposing yourself to different situations, you will improve yourself to go higher and higher. This will empower you and others to attain success.

Visit my website, thriveuncertainty.com, for bonuses.

Learn not to Worry

The majority of us did not worry when we were kids. We would climb trees, jump from tables, even behave like movie heroes without worrying what might happen. Why is it different now? You may worry about everything, even things that don't ever happen.

Is it the culture?
Is it your beliefs?
Is it yourself?
What has happened for that shift to occur?

When we become more conscious of our life and take more responsibilities, anything that could shatter our life will bring anxiety or can potentially increase anxiety if it has not yet happened. Human beings are wired for certainty, and any change that occurs in our life triggers anxiety and stress.

Recently, the Covid-19 pandemic has created lots of anxiety for millions of people worldwide. People worry because the news is full of factual information in regard to the number of deaths and people contracting the virus on a daily basis. Additionally, there's no cure and no treatment to prevent the virus. It is normal to feel anxious, but it is not healthy to chronically worry about it to the extent of depriving yourself from your routine, your passion, your creativity and living your life to the fullest.

In some cases, people worry too much and are persistently creating negative thoughts in their life, which becomes an anxiety issue. It becomes chronic, leading to insomnia, migraines, and stomach cramps, to name a few. Just remember that worrying about your particular situation will not make the problem disappear. You have to face the situation; deal with it and learn from the experience.

Change happens in many ways, good and bad. There are corporate or companies' restructurings, downsizings, lay offs, and cut backs. The good things could be promotion and upgrading. In order for a company to continue to grow, it needs continuous change. If it keeps stagnant, then there is no progress, and the company will not survive. Employees feel insecure when there are lots of changes happening in the economy as well as in their workplace, and this creates anxiety and stress. Worry is good to a certain extent as it keeps you performing to your best abilities, but at the same time it could be demotivating if you worry too much about things that you don't have control over.

Often people are terrified about restructuring as they don't know what's going to happen to them. Employees fear they can lose their job and they worry about how they will pay bills and get food on the table for themselves and their families. People are so attached to their workplace, and because they are at ease receiving their steady paycheck, they do not worry about other things.

Worry is one of the biggest problems facing humanity, and it can lead to a serious disease if it's not being taken care of.

People worry about everything. I'm sure if you have an interview next week, you will start worrying about your interview today, and you may jeopardize your first impression because of your fear. The greatest thing you can do is simply your best.

We live in a world of fierce competition and we worry a lot because we want perfection in everything we do. There's lots of pressure everywhere, whether it's at school, college, university, at the workplace, in your personal life, and so on. When you worry too much, you can spoil your life. There's tension in your life, urging you to succeed. Sometimes, its helpful and sometimes it's not.

Ask yourself these questions:

How much important is tension in your life?
Do you really need to be anxious in order to succeed, or can you be successful without having too much pressure?

These questions will help you do things aligned to your long-term goal. Some things are not worth worrying about at all. They are just trivial things.

If you go to my website thriveuncertainty.com, you will get more information about tips on learning not to worry.

The Power of Gratitude

Showing gratefulness is a great act; it is when you are showing appreciation for kindness, or being thankful for things, experiences, people, and so on.

Human beings have a very natural way of responding to crisis, both emotionally and psychologically, but the truth is that it sometimes brings more suffering to people who are stuck in their minds and don't have clarity of things. When you show appreciation toward the world, you feel better and can cope with these challenges.

When you are grateful, you find yourself with lots of positive energy and passion to move toward your goals. You see that life has more meaning and purpose than before, and you receive more and more when you give.

You cannot say that you'll only be happy if you receive something in the future, and keep waiting to be happy. You are worthy now—not just when you lose the extra pound, or gain some pounds, or when you get the promotion at your workplace, or get your dream job. Remember, you are worthy and are perfect the way you are right now.

I knew someone who always thought that she would be happy if she won the lottery or found her life partner. One day, during a dinner conversation, I asked what her perception was about happiness. I was surprised that she wasn't happy the way she was, and was waiting to win the lottery to change herself. Then she had a few free coaching sessions about being grateful and happy, and within two months, she was transformed. She is very happy now and doesn't even think about winning the lottery to be happy.

Happiness is "now." You have to be happy with what you have in this very moment, and be grateful for what you have. Be happy about your health, how you look, your smile, your weight, and everything. Don't wait to be happy for something that you don't even know will happen. Start being grateful and happy every day, and it will keep going on.

Find gratitude in everything, even when you're faced with challenges. No challenges or obstacles in life are permanent; seek any opportunities or any growth from these challenges. Be thankful that these challenges can bring you other things in life that you probably didn't expect. You can grow from them, and they can make you a better person, and can probably help you to come up with creative ideas to enhance your life.

You may also start to keep a gratitude journal, where you can write everything that you are grateful for on a regular or daily basis. It could be things such as having great health, breathing fresh air, having fresh drinking water, amongst others. Do not be too picky about gratefulness. If you are not grateful for life, you can change your perception and start appreciating everything that you take for granted. Expressing appreciation and being thankful for things that come into your life, has tremendous health benefits that you may not even know about. There has been much proof that being grateful can lower stress and depression, and bring you happiness, joy, and a healthy lifestyle. According to Happify, gratitude increases the feel-good neurotransmitters—dopamine and serotonin—and helps you deflect those negative thoughts.

It's been a few months now, and I have been grateful every morning for at least one thing. I was sick, stressed, and depressed, and my mood was always low, for several months. I wasn't even thinking of smiling, or doing things that I love, like walking, enjoying nature, and other things. I felt miserable, and needed to get back on my feet. Being grateful is not something we are born with. We don't even learn at school that we have to be grateful every day for us to receive in abundance and be happy within ourselves. You have to train your mind and thoughts to be thankful for at least one thing every day. Whether it's in the morning or in the evening, it should be part of your routine in order for you to see the positivity and the results.

There is always something to be grateful for: your health; your work; the income you receive, whether it's active or passive income; love; smiles; the people in your life; and so much more. These small acts of thankfulness are a great example of gratitude, and when you are thankful for something, the Universe gives it back to you, even though you don't ask for anything in return. Even when things don't work out well, I'm still grateful for something, and I still thank the Universe, even in this time of crisis.

Many of us are pessimists by nature, especially with so much negativity happening in this world nowadays. The Covid-19 pandemic has shaken the lives of many people worldwide, and some are still affected by this difficult situation. When people can't make ends meet but are surviving, gratitude does not even come into the picture. What if you became grateful for something, and it at least changed the perception of one thing, and you could therefore feel and be happy? Visit my website, thriveuncertainty.com, for a free coaching session.

The Transformation

Transformation doesn't happen overnight. If you really want to be successful and achieve what you want to do in the future, it's important to have a plan of action to execute this.

Change brings stress and anxiety. If you are able to manage your emotions and feelings, then you'll be able to regulate and handle the situation to build more self-confidence and self-esteem. If a similar situation were to occur later in life, you would have the resources and skills to dive into it, accept the challenges, and come back successfully. At times, you may need to be struck by something to transform your life. You may be thinking about your situation and options of how to make your life better, so that you don't lose the opportunities of doing something great or greater than your capabilities.

When you develop and cultivate a growth mindset, no matter how challenging the situation may appear, or how deep the problem is, you will be able to view these difficulties as an opportunity to grow, by using your past experiences, resources, skills, and resiliency to fight them. Having an open-minded attitude will help you have clarity of your goals and who you want to be. Once you make the commitment of changing yourself to transform to a higher-level person, you will do your best to champion any challenges that appear in the future. You will leave aside your old thoughts and beliefs, which will have no meaning to you. You will feel enthusiastic to take on this new journey to transform your life.

Covid-19 has brought lots of turbulence and disruption to the economic and financial markets, since the beginning of January 2020 until now. Some of you have found ways to unlock opportunities for new growth, while others are still wrapped up in their own world of negativity. They do not see any opportunities that could arise out of crisis. Transformation is when you rethink and alter your life to one that you really want.

Anyone can change if they are willing to, and they have the magic possibility to change themselves into who they want to be, if they concentrate on doing so. It is the same philosophy of transformation as a caterpillar's life cycle; they turn into a butterfly. We humans have more or less the same life cycle, from the womb until we reach adulthood. Every human being has the capacity to become a better person and to achieve their goals, the same way the caterpillar changes into a butterfly. The transformation is so beautiful, attractive, and colorful that everyone loves to watch a butterfly. The butterfly will be you when you change into what you want to be. So, why don't you start now by training yourself to become that beautiful butterfly?

When change happens, you may be held back by fear of the unknown; but you may want to emerge from your cocoon, shift your focus from negative to positive thinking, and live life to the fullest, using most of your potential to reach your goals. I got out of my cocoon because I was in a crisis moment. You do not have to wait for the crisis moment to change yourself. You already have the skills to transform your life. Do not procrastinate, do not wait for the right time, and do not live in the shadow of negative thinking, even though you don't know what the future will be—muster all your courage, and discover the new life ahead. Be curious to know what the future holds for you and your family, and go for it.

I can guide you to the path of transformation if you really want this. Go to my website, thriveuncertainty.com, and register for a free coaching session now.

Accept Failure

Change happens over time, and whether it's economic, political, financial, or social change, it all brings frustration and anxiety. These changes could be deployment, political imbalance, or financial or economic crisis. Unfortunately, we do not have any control over these changes, and they still affect us in different ways. Change happens because humans want to improve their conditions and create progress to build a decent life for themselves and their families. This change is within our control and can therefore be manageable. No one is perfect, and no one can say that he or she makes the perfect decisions all the time. Not every decision you make has a positive outcome. Some decisions have negative outcomes, and you have to find other ways to achieve what you haven't accomplished.

Everything that you do involves sacrifice, and also includes some sort of cost. Nothing is pleasurable all the time. You want to keep making the right decisions based on your judgment, knowledge, awareness, values and beliefs, and environment. You need to have an open mind, where you can handle and accept failure, because if you don't, then you will not go further, and you will lose many opportunities that come your way.

If you want to have a professional and long-lasting business, you need to strive hard so that you can make it work. You may be restricted in some of the plans, but that doesn't mean that it's the end of everything. Just accept it as bad news that will help motivate you to go higher and be better. Whenever your task doesn't go the way you want it to, you may feel hurt and rejected because of all the effort you put into those results. It's okay to feel like that; do not push yourself away from what you are feeling at that moment. Acknowledge these feelings of failure, and understand that you can grow and have better results by changing the path. Accept the feelings, and it will be less hurtful in the future if something similar should happen.

"I have not failed. I've just found 10,000 ways that won't work."
– Thomas Edison

Even if you fail 100 times, it doesn't matter; what's more important is that you keep going until you find the results you've been looking for. Don't worry about what other people say about your failure, because they may not have even tried what you have already done. They may envy you for all your patience and efforts that you put into your hard work. When you succeed and realize how difficult it was to get that result, you will have more trust in your abilities to keep moving forward. Once you get it, it's like having a key to open many more doors.

Always be open minded and positive about failing, because you will be able to give yourself some feedback to start all over again, or to just simply take another route toward your goals. You may ask yourself questions like:

What did I learn from this?
How can I improve myself?
What are the strategies I can use in that same process to get a better result?
What do I need to add, remove, or change to improve my learning and my process?

Remember, everything is in the learning and experiences, for you to gain knowledge and awareness. Whenever you have an emotional fallout, it is good to vent, especially to others who are already in the same business as yours. They may be able to give you their feedback and perspectives. You may also listen to some motivational speakers about their failures and how they changed that process to succeed. You will realize that you are not the only one who has failed once, twice, or thrice... there are many like you who have failed many times before they succeeded.

Remember, nothing comes easy in life; everything takes hard work.

Visit my website, thriveuncertainty.com, for bonuses. In my next chapter, you will be stunned to learn of the super power that's already within yourself, and how to make full use of this to achieve your goals.

Chapter 8

The Leader in You

"If you are a leader, you should never forget that everyone needs encouragement. And everyone who receives it-young or old, successful or less than successful, unknown or famous - is changed by it. "
- John C. Maxwell

Everyone has a talent. Don't let it die; allow it to grow, and make use of it. Sometimes you need to do a little bit of work to make yourself better, or sometimes you need more time and work than others. Anyone can be creative and work on their own, once they know what they really want to do.

Be Your Own Boss

You want to start your business, but you don't know where to start. Don't panic. You may not be the only one in that situation. There are many ways to become your own boss. You can do in-class or online courses, or use your talent to put it into practice. It may sound attractive to be your own boss; however, you need to consider some aspects of entrepreneurship.

You need to think about what you want to do: whether you want to work for yourself, work for a company, work as a freelancer, or in a partnership—it all depends on you. Once you have assessed all your market ideas, and have had a conversation with your mentor or people in the same business as yours, then you'll be able to make a decision on whether you want to make a switch. Or if you're already working somewhere, you should look at other available options. If you go to my website, thriveuncertainty.com, you'll get more ideas.

Lots of people want to be their own boss and be self-employed. However, if you are currently working and receiving a steady paycheck, it may not be prudent to jump to being your own boss. What you may do is to work on your business part-time at first, and then gradually get into full-time. Being an entrepreneur is not an easy path, and it's not a difficult path either. You need to be disciplined and committed, and able to accept failure in order to succeed. You need to bring the following components into your business:

- Skillsets
- Competence
- Knowledge
- Wisdom

After you put all your effort and your time in doing your own research work, then you will be able to make an informed decision on whether being your own boss is an option for you or not. If you do think that being your own boss is a good thing, then you will need to follow some basic steps of starting a business. Once you have your own business, you will be able to have full control. You will master your life and your financial circumstances.

Don't wait for change to happen in order to make a change in your life or think of creating your own business. Whenever you have some ideas in your mind, plan what you want to do as your career plan. Life is full of surprises, both good and bad. Bring your ideas and creativity into a business that you know you can do, even with lots of hard work. Some of you may be taking your life for granted. You may think that you get what comes along, and you don't have a plan or have set any goals for achieving your purpose. If you want to see a plan for starting a business, visit my website, thriveuncertainty.com, to register for a free coaching session.

You may have a good 9 to 5 job, but your desires are different from the work you are actually doing. You may be suffocating inside for not achieving your goals or finding your purpose or your dream job, because you are working under pressure at a company that you may not be happy with, or have any satisfaction with your job. Sometimes your co-workers may give you a headache, or the management wants different things. You may be day dreaming about your own business, and you are not performing at your current job or workplace. Life will not be interesting if you are not meeting your goals. You will feel that you are missing out on something important in your life. Don't waste more time; think and act.

If you are afraid of starting your own business, you should know that fear is a common emotion that the majority of people feel when they start something new. With any new thing you do in life, especially when you don't know what the outcome will be, you will experience fear and even anxiety because of the unknown and the risk you may take in fulfilling your dreams. But remember, if you do not take risk, then you won't know if it's worth it or not. Experiencing fear is normal, and it means that you have the determination to start your business. Never be afraid of putting your idea out there if you really want to. Success doesn't come in a day or a week; be patient, and you will see the results of your efforts.

The Attitude

Attitude is a way of thinking; it is the beliefs, feelings, and emotions about something, someone, or a particular event, which can have a powerful influence over behavior. For example, if someone is scared of change, the behavior component of how the person will react in the face of change may be avoidance or procrastination.

"You cannot control what happens to you, but you can control your attitude toward what happened to you, and in that, you will be mastering change rather than allowing it to master you."
– Brian Tracy

Life is full of ups and downs. It's a journey of expected and unexpected things. Life can be beautiful and enjoyable; and at other times, life could be filled with bad and unpleasant things. Yes, this happens to everyone, not only you. When bad things happen in your life, you have a choice of how you look at it. You may be lamenting over your bad situations, or you may take it as an experience and move on in your life, and anticipate how to deal with any similar circumstances in the future. So, you have the choice to either adopt a positive or negative perspective. The choice is yours.

It is no secret that change brings lots of frustration and stress to people. Different cultures react to change in different ways, and they may exhibit different attitudes toward change. At times, people may have an ambivalent attitude toward things or people, and this could result in conflicts within themselves and with others, as well as sometimes not having the ability to make decisions and take action. Attitude is an important factor in determining someone's success or failure and change.

In my own life experience, I've been through a lot of difficult situations. Many of you may have gone through much more than what I've been through, but we all have to face it. It's a way for us to understand how to deal with life's situations. Even the richest people on earth experience misfortunes at times in their lives. Success is not given to anyone; you have to earn it through your hard work, dedication, and commitment, like all successful people. Some may be talented but still need to work on it. You are talented too, and you need to keep doing what you love so that you can improve yourself.

Your attitude may reflect your values and beliefs; however, it may be influenced by your physical environment, your peers, social media, and even your intuition and your unconscious mind. In the early stages of life, your family, society, and traditions taught you what is and what is not acceptable in life. As you grew and learned more about life, your perspective on life may have changed to be different from what you learned a few years ago. Different stages of life teach you different things, as change happens all the time. Your attitude may change with your own perspective of life, and throughout your different learning phases of life. Your attitude will also depend on your salary, status, work, culture, and so on.

As you've heard, the Covid-19 pandemic, in the year 2020, has put lots of people into financial crisis. The financial stress is scary for lots of people around the world, and it creates anxiety, while others see opportunities to be creative and develop ideas. Your attitude—whether it's a positive or negative one, and how you react and behave—determines whether you can change the situation. It is essential to be aware of your own cultural values and beliefs, as well as intercultural differences. You need to embrace the change, stay positive, and be open to accept failure.

The ways in which you have experienced change in the past determines how you perceive change now and in the future. If the past experiences during crisis has been positive, then you will be optimistic about any future change. If it was the contrary, then you will have different views on how to deal with change in the future, and whether you will be able to or not. It is important for you to learn and grow from your failures, or else it will hold you back; you will be too scared to move forward and achieve success.

When you have high self-esteem and self-confidence, you will be able to deal with change effectively. Not only will you succeed, but you will also have the opportunity to be creative and to enhance your personal and professional growth. You may learn some tips on my website, thriveuncertainty.com.

Your Communication Skills

Communication is one of the most important life skills to learn. It is the transferring of information from one person to another or to a group of people for the understanding of a situation. There are two main types of communication: verbal or non-verbal.

Every person communicates everyday whether it is on a personal or professional level. We've all been communicating since the early days of childhood; I would rather say since the womb. There is no secret recipe for good communication. There are some basic concepts but would be helpful if everyone adopts them throughout their life.

To become a great communicator, it is important to:

- Do not use jargon
- Be respectful
- Practice active listening when others are talking
- Be open-minded of what other people have to stay
- Respect their opinions even if you do not agree with them and then you can ask questions

- Use a good body language
- Watch the tone of your voice
- Use clear and simple words to get your message across
- Be mindful of eye contact and do not stare at the other person as it can make him or her uncomfortable

No matter how busy you find yourself on a daily or regular basis, you always have to make time to communicate with others, especially those who are close to you like your partner, children, family members who you live with. When you have some ideas but unsure if they are great or not, don't hesitate to share them with those who could understand where you are going. You can get someone's feedback or suggestions or ideas of what you want to achieve.

During change, lots of people experience different types of emotions such as sadness, anxiety, fear, happiness, anger and others. It is very important to share your emotions with others you trust so that you can relieve yourself from frustration and negativity. By talking to others, you also get support and advice like you are not alone in the midst of crisis. You will get some help in managing your emotions. When you get advice and information about your situations, then you are able to make an informed decision that will help you better in handling them.

Communication plays an important role in all facets of life especially in times of crisis. It is paramount to build and maintain positive relationship with everyone through good communication. Without effective communication skills, it will be difficult to effectively construct and foster productive relationships. Communication is worldwide. Now with technology improvements such as free communication applications like WhatsApp, Skype, Zoom and so on, anyone can talk to anyone at any time anywhere. Sometimes it requires good internet to be able to connect with others

At the workplace, employees feel comfortable and heard when their perspectives are taken into consideration. If they are unable to convey their ideas due to limited communication or restrictions, then the workplace needs to improve its communication so that employees can bring new ideas that could be implemented in the future. If open communication within a workplace is encouraged, the team will be prosperous and will continue to grow. When communication is clear from the management level and is aligned with the company's directions and vision, employees feel a sense of security and belongingness to the workplace.

Visit thriveuncertainty.com for more information.

Achieve Balance

Maintaining a balanced life is becoming increasingly important in this fast-paced world. Seeking a balanced life leads you to a happy and joyful life, as it promotes your personal and professional growth. It also keeps your mental peace and well-being alive through a healthy and financially independent life.

With ongoing change in this modern world, we all get bogged down with different types of responsibilities. It is crucial to sustain a balanced diet, as well as work, fitness, and leisure activities that can help your overall health and well-being.

The definition of achieving balance differs from person to person. We all have our own cultures, traditions, and environments that influence our lifestyles, which we need to take into consideration. It is important to understand how you can maintain a balanced lifestyle for your own personal life.

One time, I met someone who worked really hard for a company, for about 12 hours daily during the week, and 7 hours on the weekend. After several months, we met again, and he was still working the same hours. I then asked him a few questions about his life and goals. We met again after several months, and he thanked me, as my questions had changed his life positively, and he now had a balanced life while still working. He had reduced his hours and now had more time to spend with his family and for himself. There is no harm in working hard, but it is important to assess your life and have a work-life balance, so that you can spend your time and effort working, and at the same time, with your family and your own personal pursuits.

If you want to bring balance to your life, there are many ways that you can achieve this. You need to understand where you are in your life and what needs to change. Look at all the aspects of your life: marital, work, financial, health, and so on. Then you can determine what needs to be changed or amended.

It doesn't matter whether you are a married, single, divorced, or in any type of relationship—achieving balance is crucial to your life. If you haven't done this yet, you need to assess your life to understand what you need to do.

You cannot change whatever is not within your control, and if you have a lot of responsibilities, whether they be personal or professional, all you need to do is to plan how to achieve them, because you cannot do everything at one time. You need to manage your time and make a priority list so that you can handle the most important things first. Sometimes it is important to know where you stand and whether you can accept other work; and if not, just say no. When you schedule time for yourself, then you will be able to have your leisure and passion embedded into your life.

Whenever you plan your week, make it a point to schedule time for yourself, your family, and your friends, and for activities that will make you happy and energize you to continue living your life. It is important to stay away from work when you are having your time off. Those of you who have a work phone, you can turn it off when you are not working, so that you don't regularly check your phone email to see what's happening at work. Avoid talking about work, or stressing yourself about work deadlines when you are not working. Keep yourself busy with activities for your own personal growth, and get moving. You can add some meditation or relaxation in your daily activities, as it helps you to recharge yourself.

You need to take care and look after yourself in order to achieve a balanced life, because if you are not healthy, then how will you be able to take care of your family or others, or even take care of your work? When you are traveling in an airplane, and if something goes wrong, you have to put on your oxygen mask first before you help your children or anyone else. If you help your children first, then you will be lacking oxygen, and you may even lose your life. Most women, with their maternal instincts, or men with paternal instincts, would try to save their children first, but they would have to remember their safety first.

Living in a world of constant change makes it difficult to know what's going to happen, or to make decisions for the short term; however, you should keep in mind that when you set long-term goals for your personal and professional life, you need to keep going until you attain success. Be willing to take risk, because it can help you to see the other side of the coin. If you don't dare to cross the street, you won't know what's on the other side. It is the same with a coin, which has two sides; so in the same way, it applies to you—it is either positive or it is not, but keep on doing it by trying different ways, until you achieve what you want in life.

Manage your Boundaries

Managing your boundaries is crucial for a healthy lifestyle and for maintaining a good relationship with anyone, whether at the personal or professional level. When you manage your boundaries, you know what comes in and what stays out. You have full control over your life, your encounters, and your surroundings. You set limits and boundaries to protect yourself and your family, be it related to anything physical, mental, emotional, spiritual, physiological, etc.

Change happens all the time at every stage of life. Do not let your boundaries be affected by change. Your values and cultures help you to determine and set your boundaries, because you have full understanding of how to figure out where to set boundaries and their limitations. In life, it is important to set your personal and professional boundaries. They should not be overlapping each other, as there would be conflict within yourself, and you would feel lost, which may have a negative impact on your health.

When you start a relationship with your life partner or your friends, it's important to set boundaries because, on many occasions, it is based on assumption or it is taken for granted. Once you set boundaries in your relationship, whether it's intimate or not, then both parties will know the limitations of the relationship, thus avoiding any conflicts that may arise.

Boundaries are crucial in a workplace environment, whether it is with your co-workers, your clients, or your management. It shows your values, culture, and work ethics. Setting defined and clear boundaries will foster healthy relationships anywhere, with anyone. Fostering boundaries increases a productive workplace environment, leading to less negativity and less conflicts.

I was raised to be kind and respectful to others, and to see this as a virtue. At my workplace, I couldn't refuse any extra work by my management, like doing the French caseload voluntarily, and other things. When my boundaries were crossed, I couldn't say anything, and it was very frustrating. So, it is important to set boundaries for which behaviors are acceptable toward you, and which are not; and most importantly, to follow through.

If the boundaries get crossed, then be assertive, especially if you are a shy person. I know, it takes lots of effort to do it, but do not be scared; it has to start somewhere.

If you are shy or unaccustomed to being assertive, take baby steps until you get used to it. You will need to practice to get better. You may perceive yourself, or be perceived, as being rude to others, but don't worry about that. What really matters is that you be firm about your boundaries, and do not allow them to be crossed. Ensure that your values and your emotions are being respected. It doesn't mean that you are being disrespectful or unkind. It simply means that you are taking care of yourself by being true to yourself and your needs. I've gone through this, and I can help you.

See my website, thriveuncertainty.com, for more details and bonuses.

If you are in a relationship and you feel that you are letting your boundaries slip, have a clear conversation with that person, and let them know how you feel and what your boundaries are, by being assertive and paying attention to your feelings. If a person crosses your boundaries and you keep quiet, this will create conflict inside you and will give rise to anger, tension, and frustration, because you're not getting what you need. This could be harmful to your health and can lead to health issues and/or burnout.

We are all cocooned in our world, where we think for ourselves and we do not pay attention to others. It's not because of being selfish; it's because we are so busy in life that we do not have time for others. So, it is important for you to tell others what your boundaries are so that they know. Assertiveness will help you a lot with your own rights, needs, and boundaries, while taking into consideration others' needs. When you're assertive, you get your point across firmly and fairly—not aggressively but empathetically. If you find yourself struggling to establish boundaries, go to thriveuncertainty.com, where you will get some tips about setting boundaries.

Have No Expectations

It is a blissful experience when you live your life with no expectations. We all live with expectations of ourselves, our children, our families, our friends, and so on. When our expectations are not met, it creates fear and frustration. When you don't have any expectations in life, then you live without worry or fear of what may not happen as a result.

It is good to have expectations in life for yourself, but it is not healthy to expect anything in return for something that you do for others. You will experience more peace and happiness when you don't expect anything in return. When you help someone in need or do someone a favor, do not expect to have something in return. Do not expect to get anything from anyone, not even those that are close to you. If you have expectations of people that you help, then when these expectations are not met, it will only bring suffering, anger, irritation, and sadness to you.

People have lots of expectations in general. If you focus your life on not expecting anything in return, you will live a happy and healthy life. It is not easy to let go of expectations, but it is possible. If you are a child, you have the expectation that your parent will buy you everything you want. Well, this is not necessarily true, because they are there to guide and protect you so that you can become financially independent, or simply independent.

We live in a fast-paced world where everything keeps moving, and we don't even know what's changing on a daily basis. Once you take responsibility for yourself and your actions, you will notice that you no longer have to worry or be irritated by others. When you no longer feel angry or sad, then your mind will be focusing on other things that have more importance in your life.

It is not because you helped your siblings earlier that now they have to help you. It may be that they also are in a critical situation where they need help, but they are not asking for any. Do not allow your emotions to irritate you, spoil your mood, or affect your surroundings. When you have no expectations of others, you happily help others. It works the same way when you buy a lottery ticket; you expect to win the jackpot. Think about all the people that are buying lottery tickets with that same expectation. What's your chance of winning the lottery— it's minimum, right? I cannot tell you to buy the lottery ticket without having any expectations because, basically, that's why we buy lottery tickets—with the expectation to win the lottery. Do not allow yourself to be emotionally attached to something that's not even within your control.

When you have no expectations from others, there's no room for disappointment or resentment. You live your life freely, without any guilt or owing someone a favor, nor do you feel that someone owes you a favor. You will focus your mind on positive things, or things that align with your goals.

As parents, we have expectations that our children will act in certain ways, do certain things at certain times, behave in certain ways, and dress accordingly to our choices. At times, we even think about what career they should be doing, instead of the children thinking for themselves. In certain cultures, it's the parents who choose the bride or groom for their children, because they have expectations. They think about their traditions, culture, and society. Every culture is different; there's no good or bad.

No one is perfect. If you expect to do everything right all the time, you are destined to feel stress when things don't go as expected. When you are ambitious and want to achieve many things at the same time, and when it doesn't happen the way you expect it to, you feel stressed and overwhelmed; you lose trust in yourself, and you feel like quitting. Just know that no one is perfect, and allow yourself to make mistakes. Things don't always go as we plan; this is a fact of life, and we have to accept it.

I had a friend who used to surprise me with good things, and it was always a pleasure to receive these things; not because of the fact that I was getting something, but because I wasn't expecting anything. I would always get things, even without asking, and I remember how happy I would be, because I had no expectations.

Every year for my birthday, my mom would bake a cake with lots of decorations, or my brothers or relatives would buy me a cake. I always expected a nice birthday cake, until I immigrated to Canada by myself. For my birthday, in Canada, I was all alone, and I was sad that my close ones were not in Canada. That day, I had training, and they had a birthday cake and sang for me and so on, which I wasn't expecting, and it made me feel really happy.

When we don't have expectations, anything we receive brings happiness. On the other hand, when we have expectations from others, we limit ourselves to live happily and fully. I also understood that those who really cared for me were hundreds of miles away, and they could not give me any cake because of the distance between us. Little by little, I changed from having expectations to having no expectations, and I could feel and see my life changing for the better.

If you want to live a happier life, then from now on, you must try hard not to have expectations of anyone, not even your life partner, your parents, your children, your closest friends, or those at your workplace. It will definitely be hard at the beginning to reduce your level of expectations of others, but with perseverance, you will see how free and happy you will feel by having no expectations. Go to my website, thriveuncertainty.com, for bonus information.

Recognitions and Rewards

Reward is a good initiative to motivate someone to perform better, to take action, and to live a better life. When you reward yourself, your brain releases dopamine, which is very important and plays a major role in your life. You feel good, cheerful, and happy. It also promotes your well-being, and elevates your self-esteem and self-confidence.

It is important to recognize and appreciate the good work of others, because they take the time to execute their tasks. It is good when a child is encouraged to do some work and is rewarded for the completion of the good work, from a very young age. It helps the child to grow into a responsible person when they take responsibilities, be accountable for their mistakes, and learn from them.

When I lost my dad, I was pretty young. I remember that my mom had never worked before, and because my brothers and I were very young, my mother started to work so that my siblings and I could finish school. My younger brother had just completed kindergarten. Life was not easy, and the only income that my mother was receiving at the time was the widow's pension, which was barely nothing. There was no social assistance or children's assistance to help my mother raise the kids. She worked really hard so that we could go to school. All her efforts were rewarded, as my siblings and I were able to complete high school, and some of us finished university. My two elder brothers were very intelligent, but due to a lack of finances, they didn't get the opportunity to go to university. They all obtained good results from their high school certificates, but going to university was very expensive, and they couldn't afford it.

During change, there are lots of people who mobilize to help the community and those in need. Change is everywhere, and it can either have a positive or negative impact on communities, people, and the wildlife. At times, natural disasters bring change and leave an impact on people and society and the universe. The bushfires in Australia, from September 2019 to March 2020, were devastating to the wildlife, and billions of animals were affected.

If you are the only one working to financially support your family, don't forget to reward yourself from time to time. It's not about buying something expensive; you can do it with simple things, such as a stay-at-home movie night, buying a fancy pot of coffee, hot chocolate, or tea, or treating yourself with a nice candlelit dinner, or anything that you cherish. You can also go on a hike, go for a bike ride, or relax on a beach. There are many ways that you can reward yourself, as well as your family for their accomplishments. Some may cost you money and others are free. You can go to thriveuncertainty.com to see a full list of ways to reward yourself.

If you are an entrepreneur and you have your own business, don't just keep working hours and hours without taking a break. Take some time off and enjoy some mini breaks to relax, and then get back to work. You will be more productive when you take some time off to reward yourself for your accomplishments. The more you reward yourself, the more effort you will put in to achieve more.

At the work place, when employees are doing a really good job, they sometimes get promotions, or they could even be redeployed when there is a need for their service or their expertise. Change can be positive or negative; even a promotion can be a positive or negative thing. Most of the time, a promotion means a lot of more work to accomplish, having to supervise people, or simply a change of work. A promotion can also be regarded as a reward for doing a good job at the workplace, or anywhere. If you are dedicated to your work or your own business, the outcome will be rewarding. Recognizing and rewarding your employees effectively is very important, as it promotes engagement and retains the employees for a longer time. Lots of employees work overtime, and they work harder to keep the workload low, because they want to accomplish their work in a timely manner.

If you have children, you may think that it's their responsibility to make their beds, clean their bedrooms, and so on. If you do not teach them, they will not learn it by themselves. The more you reward a child, the more things they will want to learn and acquire as knowledge, which will eventually help them in their life. A child will learn more at a young age. When a child is rewarded, this is an incentive or a reinforcement that he/she can learn something or do a good deed, instead of doing bad things, which will result in punishment. These positive actions will reinforce achieving what you want later on in life. When you achieve your goals, it is important to reward yourself before you go to the next step. If you are faced with change and you feel discouraged, then you can relate to the reward of your past achievement, and you can be motivated to carry on with your present tasks.

Some of you reading this book may fall into the category of procrastinators. This is a good tip for you, to stop procrastination and reward yourself when you complete a goal. Take a moment to feel happy about your accomplishment, and reward yourself because you well deserve it. When you feel happy about completing a task, and you reward yourself, you'll be motivated to do the next step until you reach your goals. There is no guilt in rewarding yourself for completing a task.

There are many reasons why you do certain things and why you don't do certain things. Sometimes you are motivated to act in a certain way or perform certain things because of your internal desires and wishes to do something; but other times, you may be willing to complete a task only because of the reward attached to it. Remember, there is no harm if your behavior is motivated by a reward. You may practice singing to be in the final competition. So, your reward is to be elected in the finals. And as you can see, there is no harm in practicing singing every day.

Visit my website, thriveuncertainty.com, for more information.

About the Author

Karuna Narain was born and raised in Mauritius, and she immigrated to Canada a few years ago. She is very supportive and caring, and is an excellent leader.

Karuna has devoted her life to helping the vulnerable and those in need. Through her devotion as a social worker, Karuna has been able to positively transform the lives of many students, families, and those who suffer from concurrent disorders, and young people that are going through difficult times.

Karuna has displayed a keen sense of commitment and dedication to the cause of development of the community, as an outstanding social worker. She has been awarded two National Youth Leadership Awards, jointly with the Ministry of Youth and Sports, in Mauritius.

Karuna loves to upgrade herself through continuous learning and aligning her goals and vision. She has brought her knowledge and support to many people who've been physically, mentally, or emotionally challenged. Karuna has been a blessing on many occasions to people she helped.

Karuna inspires, empowers, and guides people to live their well-deserved lives and to achieve what they want. She has helped lots of people achieve what they desire the most. She has a passion for what she does, and will transform your life. If you would like to have her as your coach, please go to her website, thriveuncertainty.com, and notify her. She would be happy to give you a free half-hour coaching session.

Karuna is also available for delivering keynote presentations to appropriate audiences. For rates and availability, please contact the author at: **karuna.narain5@gmail.com.**

www.ingramcontent.com/pod-product-compliance
Lightning Source LLC
Chambersburg PA
CBHW071955090426
42740CB00011B/1952